Dear Old Friends

A loving reminder that the band won't stop playing
till you stop dancing. Xo, Jim

James B. Flaherty

Enjoy! XO Jim Flaherty

Free Gift

Interested in a Free Gift that can Change your Life?

What does the www mean in Website addresses? Warm, Wise & Witty? That's not bad. Now I have a bunch of worthwhile websites that are Wonderful, Welcoming & Worth It. I know, I know, deep diving into the Website World is about as much fun as swimming with sharks. Or if you can remember far enough back, like the first time you had to take algebra in school! Aaarrgh!

But not to worry. I've done your homework for you. I've looked at too many websites to count and narrowed them down to a manageable group I think you'll find interesting and valuable. Oh, maybe you won't use all of them, but a lot of them have something that will help make all your tomorrow's terrific.

Okay, you ask, how do I get my hands on these virtual pots of gold? Easy. There's a link at the bottom of this page. You move your mouse, or your finger, and click on that link and you'll have a blank email addressed to me, at: talktome@jamesbflaherty.com and you send me a note saying something nice, like, All right, Jim, cough up those warm, wise, witty, wonderful, welcoming and worth it websites, right now. Well, you don't have to say all that, just a simple, Send me Your Favorite Websites, Jim. I want to have a Love Affair with Life, and be as happy as you are when I wake up every day.

So come on, friend. Click the link. I can't wait to hear from you.

https://www.subscribepage.com/dearoldfriends

Xo, Jim

TABLE OF CONTENTS

I dedicate this book to very dear (and departed) friends, Honor and Carl Tranum. You'll meet them (and I know you'll love them as I did) in the pages ahead.

Chapter One

HOW IT ALL BEGAN

"The body does get older, but the person gets smarter." --- Burl Ives

OH, I WISH BURL was right. And what's that other "oh yeah?" expression: "Old Enough to Know Better" Hmm, wish it were true. I'd like to think it is. Anyway, this little book or memoir or diary or whatever you choose to call it, was something I wrote, maybe 44 years ago. You may ask, what have you been doing with it for the past 45 years—editing?

So, you're going to read how I was feeling back then in my prime, around 42 years old (I thought 50 to 75 were my best years), with up-to-the-minute commentary and additions by an 86-year-old (mentally going on 66). Anyway, thought you should know this book took me 42+ years to complete. Now and then I'll remind you, so you'll know whether it's a young whippersnapper talking or a wise (I'm laughing at myself) elderly senior.

This originally was a love letter. It was Me saying Thank you Thank you Thank you for your love and guidance and tolerance, thinking of my Dear Old Friends, many 30 or 40 years older, who injected me with the juice of human kindness and caring. They were all people who welcomed every day as another blessing, another opportunity to learn, teach, create, console, uplift—God, they were amazing, and why I was so privileged to be embraced by their wisdom still astounds me.

Trust me when I tell you age 86 is not a picnic in the park. But it also is not like driving into the heart of a hurricane or tornado, or I can't imagine living in a true war zone. However, it has forced me to look at the many challenges of aging and to figure out how to not surrender to its physical, mental, and emotional demands. And dammit, pardon me, darn it, please listen to me, and stop thinking about surrendering yourself!

First, I'll tell you who I am. I doubt if it will make your heartbeat faster, but you should understand who's writing these words. Okay? I am remarkably neat, clean, and disciplined. Even though I have a full-time housekeeper/cook (we call her our Nanny) living in, I roll out of bed (and I'm 86 years old) and turn around and make my bed. I then go to my pool and exercise, doing 1200 high knee jogs in shoulder deep water, then back upstairs for soapy shower and clean clothes, followed by my everyday perfect breakfast—a double portion of fresh cut-up fruit, with a healthy helping of homemade applesauce on top, and sometimes a crunchy healthy cereal on top.

Next, 15 steps up to my balcony office, where my desk often looks like a herd of wild hogs just ran across it, had a party acting irresponsibly, and ran off. When I can't tolerate the clutter another minute, I spend a day cleaning the desk down to the bone, which entails filing (I miss the luxury of having a full-time secretary). But I'm drifting away from this document. Whilst cleaning recently, and looking at files in a secondary filing cabinet, I FOUND THIS BOOK, OR WHATEVER THE HELL YOU WANT TO CALL IT. I was shocked! How could I have written a 110-page document and forgotten it? Was life that demanding? I guess so, or at least I thought it was.

I was a pushy kid. Oh, not in the obnoxious sense of the word. Our pre-drug, pre-electronics generation was not as difficult as today's youth. I was just hyper-active, and boiling-over with the need to be helpful, to take part, to share my life and thoughts with everyone who touched my life. I guess it was back then that my special relationship began with an older generation.

Maybe one of my first "older" friends was Jane Prettyman, my high school biology teacher. I was 15 and I suppose Jane was an ancient 45. I fell under her brilliant tutelage for just four years. It turns out Jane had dated my father before he met and married my darling mother, whom you will meet later in this book. And it was Jane, a brilliant teacher with some serious personal issues, who laid her own problems aside to help comfort me. I was drowning in a quicksand of self-pity on a hot South Florida afternoon in 1950 when the only air-conditioning available was in movie theatres and millionaire's homes. That same year, my wonderful, loved-by-everyone Father died, only 47 years old.

Jane told me, whilst wallowing in my cloak of Poor Me that steamy afternoon, *"Now listen to me, James. I know your sorrow about your father is real and deep, but your loss is nothing compared to your mother's. She has lost her lover."* Slightly prudish (I still have an untraceable strain of Victorianism in me), I was surprised by the intensity of her words, but they stayed with me, and I remember that moment now as if it were yesterday. So, Jane became my first "older" friend.

That allegiance to "older" has followed me throughout my life. For the moment, I'm going to set my mother and parents aside, because your parental relationship often has too many facets to be a clear-cut friendship. When age irons out your Mother/Son/Father/Daughter relationships and you allow yourselves to function as just people, it can be magical. I'll speak long and lovingly of this phenomenon when we reach the chapter entitled, Mom and Me. And when I get there, remind me to talk about Daughters and Me, which is one of the great Happy Cloaks I get to wear every day.

I realized when I was still in my 20s that my Dear Old Friends were crucial to my personal outlook, my career, almost every decision I made. Maybe I should say Dear "Older" Friends, because they were 20 to 50 years older than I, and advised, criticized, questioned, supported, and loved me as I tiptoed (and stomped) my way through that marvelous maze call Life. In short, they took a middle-class boy who doubted his ability to end up in the corner office and made it good to be Jim. I think they're the reason I was chosen as Master of Ceremonies for my 30th, 40th and 50th High School Reunions.

And while thinking about them pushing and poking and hugging me, I started writing this love letter to them and about them—44 years ago. Huh? Yeah, I wrote the first draft of Dear Old Friends 44 years ago, and just this year, realizing I had become a Dear Old Friend to quite a few kids between 20 and 50, finished writing my Dear

Old Friends with a memoir thanking them for having my back.

And whether you're 25, or 45, or anywhere up to 86 (My Age at publication time), I think you'll find some very solid ideas about staying crucial to yourself—and everyone else. Remember, the band won't stop playing till you stop dancing!

Recently, (this was a note from 1977) a dear and beautiful friend of mine—Ruth West by name, annoyed that her body had reached 80 when her mind was still about 40, or maybe 39 is nicer for a lady—-said to me: *"You put no age on people do you, Jim? You just accept them as people, as your mental and physical equal, even if you have to make allowances for them."* Ruth thanked me for making the past two years, difficult ones, easier for her. And I thought how dear of her to say it, but I didn't really do anything. I mean, we were friends, chums, and surely, I benefitted as much, if not more, from her friendship as she did from mine.

This personal involvement with an older, wiser, more settled generation has comforted me and guided me through most of a satisfying and productive life. There were countless people I could name who would be astounded at the importance of their influence on my every thought, every action. They were cornerstones of calm, beacons in a stormy sea of humanity. People, who I am sure, just thought we were friends for the moment, a few hours, weeks, or months, not necessarily a lifetime? Perhaps they were neighbors, or friends of my parents, or bosses, or co-workers. They taught me how to live.

I'm remembering gentle Howard Moss and his irascible Helen, whose razor-sharp voice and strident exclamations couldn't hide the tender pushover she really was. They made it possible for my wife and I to enjoy country life many weekends with them, inviting us even though we had young, active children.

When I bought a brownstone in NYC, they were there to advise me. They introduced me to the wonderment of Alcoholics Anonymous, (even though I wasn't a candidate way back then). It was the first time I was ever aware of someone being and admitting they were alcoholic. That friendship lasted 25 years!

Then there were bosses who shaped my life, if but for a few minutes, some stayed with me through the years. I remember beautiful Dorothil Patterson, a deeply religious Christian Scientist, who wore flowered hats and had a Gene Tierney overbite. Her femininity and charm made me flirt (not seriously, remember I was and still am a wee bit prudish) which would make her blush. We exchanged many, many letters, and years later, when she was dying of cancer, she was astounded and pleased she had helped me find my path. And it's true--some of my management techniques today harken back to that appealing and attractive woman, playing no favorites, injecting energy into her charges every day.

(It's 2020, and I'm remembering): In 1978, comfortably ensconced in a hard driving, but interesting corner office creative director's job in a New York City advertising agency, I was to make a decision that would have a profound effect on my life.

With one partner, a brilliant renaissance talent I might add, I purchased a decaying stack of abandoned stone, an English country estate in Amenia, New York, with forgotten grounds and gardens, just five minutes from our country home in Sharon, Connecticut. It had no glass in the windows, no working electricity, plumbing, or heating. I loved it. Troutbeck had been a glorious home in its day, a gathering place for the literati and liberals of the 1920s.

It was first settled and named in the late 1700s by the Benton family, English immigrants who named it after their native home, Troutbeck, a beautiful village in the lake district of England. An aristocratic American Jewish family--Joel Elias Spingarn and his wife, Amy Einstein Spingarn purchased the original home, which had evolved over the years into a handsome Dutch reformation farmhouse, in 1904. It burned to the ground about 1915--no injuries. Between 1916 and 1918, Amy Spingarn, Joel (Colonel Spingarn) being away at war, created a new Troutbeck with an English architect at her side, and it was this Troutbeck that ignited my passion.

With stone walls nearly two feet thick and a slate-on-slate roof that glistens in sunlight, Troutbeck is a romantic reminder of an earlier period when great homes dotted the landscape of the world.

In time, (Hah, it was a full year!) we cleaned up the debris of 35 years of emptiness, replaced plumbing and electric, built new bathrooms, a new kitchen, decorated it (we were shooting from the hip, weren't professionals at any of those tasks) and opened Troutbeck as an executive retreat and country inn. I'm happy to say we became quite well known in both categories.

But during the negotiation period to buy the property, the deal fell through because the owner was greedy, or his lawyer was being ridiculous. After much unnecessary back and forth, I called our attorney and put the kibosh on the deal. I recall telling him, "No more, Stanley, these people are nuts and I can't be pushed any farther." He did as I instructed, and although it pained me, I was and am a great believer that life goes on--that if you don't get what you want, there must be a reason, there will be other roads to travel, other doors to open, and I set about putting that fantasy country castle out of my mind.

(I realize this section is part 1977, part 2021…don't go away, this long story does have something to do with my relationship with an older generation). The day after I ended my dreamy affair with the romantic stack of stone, my attorney called to say there was a gentleman in his office and that he and the gentleman wanted to come over to my office for a chat. An unusual request from my conservative attorney. An hour later, Stan arrived with a handsome 72-year-old named Carl Tranum.

I was going to devote an entire chapter to Carl and his beloved wife, Honor, whom I am fortunate to still count as one of my nearest and dearest, but decided it might prove to be too personal, and maybe even too sad. (I wrote those words over 40 years ago.)

After putting the purchase of Troutbeck back on track (Carl accomplished that with two phone calls, his deep melodious voice still touched with a faint hint of his Tennessee boyhood) we began what would prove to be one of the most meaningful relationships of my life. Carl's wife, Honor Spingarn, was a gifted painter and intellectual, a beautiful, gracious woman who had grown up in Troutbeck and New York City. She had studied art with Hoffman in Germany and was very much a product of an upper-class New York family.

It was Honor who first opened the door to friendship. When she and Carl would come up to New York from St. Thomas in the Virgin Islands, where they had lived many years, they would call and invite me to dinner to tell them about "my Troutbeck". I welcomed any opportunity to be with them. Remember the kind of kid I had been, I still was at age 42--eager to share my experiences; willing to have my life touched by an interesting elder. Honor and Carl and I did this with open arms and much laughter, none of us sensing the passionate willingness to become "best friends" that was waiting just below the surface.

We talked, mainly Honor and I carrying the conversational ball. In the beginning, Carl was always a little wary—he was biding his time, appraising my viability as a human being. At some given moment, Carl joined this tight little klatch Honor and I had formed. Honor, knowing Carl's need for a close friend now that the physical and mental passions of business had passed him by, was grateful to see Carl and I ignore our 35-year age difference and fall into each other's heads. God, I loved Carl. Even now, remembering him, tears come to my eyes. We talked for hours—often in print. We could both afford to speak every day on the phone, but it seemed more important to put it down in writing.

I still love to write letters to the people I care about. And computers and email have made that a delightfully easy duty, not a chore.

Those first two years of Troutbeck were fraught with horrors. First, we had to restore the inner workings of the structure, clean and restore the grounds, decorate the interior, and start the marketing process. Mind you, we practically had to invent the town of Amenia—it didn't exist to anyone out of the area. "Where are you— Anemia? Amnesia?"

Then, remember, we had no experience in hospitality. We had to teach ourselves how to run a conference center and country inn and restaurant and wedding site. And imagine the problem of finding and training employees from a group of small towns. There wasn't a rich labor force, and no one had hotel or inn experience. Put it all together and Wow! I'm surprised I'm still standing. On top of that, I had to keep my brilliant but eternally anxious partner on an even keel.

Meanwhile, so we'd have enough money to pay salaries, I continued working full time in New York City. The combination of all that, plus maintaining a working and loving relationship with my two daughters, and a good and supportive friendship with an ex-wife, plus the worry of an aging mother—well, it's good I was in my young 40s not young 80s.

But what really helped was my loving relationship with Carl and Honor. I had a pretty good fix on myself. I mean, I did "Jim" pretty well, was reasonably happy with being me. But Friend Carl gave me a gift for the rest of my life. He made it great to be Jim. He made me feel secure with my instincts. He made me happy with the hand I was dealt.

We had only four years attached at the hip and heart and mind before he died. The last summer was terrible. He had cobalt every day, and Honor and I cajoled him to eat something every evening. We were his cheerleaders. We both loved him and never for a moment accepted the possibility of Carl leaving us. Dear sweet Carl. It is to Carl & his beloved Honor that I dedicate this book.

Obviously, I had many "older" friends before the joy of having Carl and Honor in my life. But I suspect it was the intensity of my friendship with them that made me reflect on all that I had gained because "I didn't put an age on people". It was my closeness to them as friends, not just as parent figures, which made me see the damnable aspects of aging.

I've always been young. Raised in a proper, intelligent middle-class home by loving and supportive parents, I didn't have terrible harsh realities of life flung at me, forcing me to become street smart, as are so many youngsters these days. Other than my father's death when I was only 14 (going on 12 emotionally), life was good.

Blessed with energy genes from my mother, who in her late 7O's didn't take naps, continued painting and teaching painting, I bounced through a happy ulcer-free career in ulcer-ridden advertising. And since I had the energy of two 25-year-olds, always felt very young. It shocks me to look in the mirror and see a 43-year-old staring back. (If you think it shocked me *back then, at age 42,* when I first wrote this book, imagine the coma I go into now at age 86--when the mirror is not—nor should it ever be—a friend!) I made these comments about myself when I was 42. "Where did my hair go? Why is the rest of it white? Thank God for good skin, the lines are minimal, and the skin tone is good". Back to age 86: Not smoking or drinking helps, watching my weight helps, but golly gee, I'm not young anymore. Could it be I'm aging? Or have I already aged?

Will the time come when my greatest joy is a smiling 50-year-old who doesn't put "age" on people and is happy to share his joys and concerns with me? It's still hard for me to accept that as a probable reality, yet I know it's true, and in fact, is happening these days. I'm impressed I was that thoughtful 40+ years ago, but I STILL feel the same way about age. . . sort of. And I'm still pushing myself harder than ever, terrified my energy source will dry up. Friend Carl told me it doesn't dry up until you want it to.

Back to the original 44-year-old manuscript: So, I write and inn-keep and still put in an 18-hour day, trying to build in enough time "to smell the roses." My sweet friend, Honor, who still (slowly) jogs two miles every morning, now in her mid-seventies, modeled a tee-shirt someone had gifted her as a gag. It said: Old Age Isn't for Sissies. Truer words never spoken. But she knows and I know, and all my ageless friends know, that although you can't stop the aging process, you sure as hell can go right on living up to the last second. You can still create, still produce, still influence, still teach, still love, and instill love. And that's what we're going to do, friends. Now, sit back, and start figuring out what you're doing right or wrong and how to make everything work out for the best. *IT'S NEVER TOO LATE TO MAKE YOUR LIFE AND THE LIVES OF THOSE AROUND YOU, BETTER, HAPPIER, MORE SATISFYING.*

I hope, through the chapters of this book, that you will become one of my Dear Old Friends. And unlike the consistently loveable Lucille Ball, who said, "The secret of staying young is to live honestly, eat slowly and lie about your age…." I want to remind you of some exciting elders who were much too busy to ever lie about their age.

Chapter Two

ROLE MODELS

"The hardest years are those between 10 and 80." — Helen Hays at age 83

L ISTEN. THE BAND IS playing Hail to the Chief. Everyone is standing up to view The Man of this or any Year. And there he is—a 74-year-old? Come on. Isn't the U.S. the biggest proponent of the youth movement? Sure we are. But we're also smart enough to recognize mature guidance. *(Remember President Reagan—he seemed so uncomplicated compared to our modern-day oval office tenants.)* Good for Ronnie. What a good example for all of us. He had enough bucks to be loafing on his ranch in California. Instead, he's got the toughest job in the world—and doing very well with it. Even handling a would-be assassin's bullet with mature ease, i.e., "Honey, I forgot to duck."

These were the people I thought about back when I was in my 40s. Let's all get realistic for a few hard minutes. Even though, like my Uncle Roger, whom you'll meet later, we may not accept the idea of leaving this earth to go to our glory, we can intellectually accept the probability of it happening someday. But what are we doing meanwhile? If we toss in the towel and say, "well, that's it—I'm old, over the hill, on the way out", then of course we are—old, over the hill and on the way out.

So, let's just take a brief look at some well-known people who are still doing what they do, still creating, still contributing right up to the last second, or, if they've departed this earthly world, left with unending applause and thanks for their early performance.

Charlie Chaplin was born in 1889 and fathered his 10th child when he was 73. Julia Child was born in 1912 and never cooked until after her 34th birthday. (That isn't wine she drinks on her TV show.) When Agatha Christie was 82, she published her 82nd book.

Claudette Colbert, born in 1907, and still beautiful, is still on Broadway in 1985. Once columnist Hy Gardner interviewed the graceful Ms. Colbert. It went something like this: Q: What keeps you looking and feeling so young? A: Not worrying about looking and feeling so young. Q: What kind of sleep do you get? A: I don't know. I'm asleep at the time. Q: What do you worry about most? A: I devote the same amount of worry to everything. Q: Do you take exercise? A: My dog walks me twice a day. Q: Do you use alcohol? A: Only in my drinks. Q: Are you bitter about anything? A: No, but I'm open to suggestions. Q: Do you ever expect to retire? A: Don't call after midnight.

More you want? More you get. Al Capp, who brought us the charms of Lil' Abner, lost a leg at age 9, and was still a popular outspoken lecturer in his 70s. Marc Chagall, born in 1887, continued to create his fantasy paintings when he was 80. And didn't we all love Benny Kubelsky, born in 1894, who went on working until he was 80. Perhaps you remember him best as Jack Benny.

Pablo Casals, who brought the cello to the absolute pitch of perfection, entertained royalty and was still walking the sands of his beloved Puerto Rico up to the end. When was that? He was 96. Remember the first prime minister of Israel, David Ben-Gurion? He continued to be a world influence right up to his demise, age 87.

The fashion world will always remember with total admiration the influence of Gabrielle Chanel--"Coco".

At age 73 she won the American Neiman Marcus Award for Fashion, and Katharine Hepburn, hardly a chicken herself, immortalized Madame Chanel in the Broadway musical, "Coco." Katharine also had a smiling comment about age: "If you survive long enough, you're revered —rather like an old building."

Getting the idea? These people had a special option in life that isn't true for all of us. They didn't really have to do any more. They had enough income, enough property, enough fame. But their interest in life, love of living, their need to enrich the human arena kept them working, creating, thinking, leading, performing. It's good for us to think of them. Let's meet some more role models.

The world will never forget Nikita Khrushchev. That old rascal was born in 1894, and as you know, continued to bang his shoe on international peace treaty desks right up to the end. J. Edgar Hoover, who served four American presidents, was born on New Year's Day in 1895, and was still unmasking communist influences in our country well into his 70s. Eamon (Gaelic for Edward) de Valera, the Irish nationalist leader, was president of the Republic of Ireland from 1959 to 1973 —when he was 90! Walter Lippmann was still an influential columnist, editor, and author in his 80s.

Samuel Goldfish, better known as Sam Goldwyn, hung around this planet until his 91st year, still speaking broken English, and still a major influence in the movie world. Maurice Chevalier was still dancing and singing in his 80s; John Ford (originally Sean O'Feeney) was still directing in his 70s, and won 4 academy awards; Dame Gladys Cooper, a marvel to watch on stage, was in her 80s when she took her last curtain call.

Duke Ellington's music was charming us when he was 75; Graham Greene was still producing books in his 70s; Buckminster Fuller, engineer, inventor, philosopher, author, published his last book when he was 80; Ira Gershwin, a magical lyricist, updated some songs for "My One and Only" in his 85th year.

Gloria Swanson wrote her autobiography in her 81st year; and quiet Bess Truman lived enough years to see her husband's name vindicated and recognized as a great American President. She was 97 when she checked out. Conrad Hilton, born in 1887, was still opening new doors in his 80s.

George Abbott is one miracle of the American theatre. Born in 1887, he has still been directing shows in the 1980s. He's remembered best for Pal Joey, On The Town, Call Me Madam, Damn Yankees, Pajama Game, Fiorello, and A Funny Thing Happened on the Way to the Forum.

And you, Friend, what are you doing these days?

Mind you, they were living and producing and creating way into their 7th, $8^{th,}$ or 9th decade. And of course, medicines and doctors weren't as smart and developed as they are today, so people are living longer. People—that's you, remember?

Let's just look at birth-dates of some other newsworthy people you know: Averell Harriman, 189 1, advisor to four presidents; Cary Grant, 1904 ; Dewitt & Lila Wallace, the founders of Reader's Digest , both in 1889; Martha Graham, 1894—the greatest influence on modern dance; Arthur Fiedler, 1894, was still directing the Boston Pops in his 80s; Joe Di Maggio, 1914; John Wayne, 1907; Lynn Fontanne, 1897; Arthur Godfrey, 1908; Jack Dempsey, 1895; Marian Anderson, 1902; Elias Canetti, 1905—won the 1981 Nobel Prize in Literature; Willem Johan Kolff, a dear and glorious physician, 1911, who has brought us artificial hearts— all since 1981, when he was 70. Claude Pepper, the oldest member of congress, was born in 1900, and went to the Senate in 1936.

More? Okay! Roy Rogers, despite a triple cardiac bypass in 1978, continued hunting, fishing, and running his restaurant chain. Colonel Sanders of Kentucky Fried Chicken fame was born in 1890. At age 65 he went on the road, sleeping in his car, convincing restaurant owners to try his unique recipe. Adele Simpson was still designing at 70; Rosalind Russell, besides her superb acting talents, was on the world's best dressed list, well into her 70s; Marianne Moore, the poet, continued creating into her 80s.

Dean Acheson was 78 when he stopped serving his government; and being a full-time soldier for 40 years didn't keep General Omar Bradley from living 88 years. Juan Trippe, a founder of Pan Am, revolutionized the airline industry. When he died at age 82, he was in the final stages of developing a flying ophthalmological laboratory for third-world countries.

It doesn't hurt us to know some more of these doers. For example, Taylor Caldwell, born in 1900, has given us more good reading than anyone can imagine. This lovely, refined woman had herself hypnotized and put in a trance at age 72. Even though the hypnotist said it revealed she had led many prior lives, she didn't believe it—but said it was an interesting experience and would use it as grist for a new book.

Let's reflect on her reaction for a moment. She embraced flexibility. Do you? If you could do something that is legal, and not life-threatening, do it—it could have a profound influence on the way you think and react to other people. It's very easy as we get older to become more rigid—physically and mentally.

Along with Claudette Colbert on Broadway in 1985, we also saw the eloquent, elegant Rex Harrison, besides siring two sons in his 60s, still over-whelming a stage with his magnetic presence. Remember funny George

Jessel? Born in 1898, he was still toasting and roasting people in the 1970s. [1] Jacques Cousteau, born in 1910, was still exploring new depths in his 7O's. There's a modern version of that action in this year's new "oldie" movie, Cocoon.

Are you feeling lazy? Now listen to me. These people weren't just blessed with perfect health. They suffered from all the aches and pains you suffer. The only difference is that most of them were-and-are too busy to dwell on the negative aspects of aging. They know every day presents yet another chance to "Go for it", another opportunity to have a productive, constructive day.

Well, that's easy for them you say--she knows how to sing, he paints, he plays cello, he or she is a writer. True. Some of them have some exceptional skills. And perhaps you're not in a position where you can change the world. But you can light one candle. It's a whole lot better than darkness. You can make someone else's life better. Or you can teach yourself to be better, to be more creative, to be smarter. Every day is a gift--use it.

I loved George Burns (I'm smiling, just thinking of him) who lived to 100. He had a couple of funnies: "I should have been a country western singer—I'm older than most western countries." Also, "If you live to the age of a hundred, you have it made, because very few people die past the age of a hundred."

But I also want you to make your own list of role models. Maybe you'll make up the list from the people I've mentioned in this chapter. Or hopefully you can compile a more personal list. You know, your brother whom you've always admired; your neighbor who's still tending her garden at age 88; your wonderful mother or grandmother (and don't forget your terrific mother-in-law) who lived forever. People you and everyone around them loved.

I want you to physically make that list and put it someplace where you'll see it every day. Your bathroom mirror is a good spot. Every morning look at the list and say to yourself, "I can be like that. I can do more with my life." Then sit down and make a list of what you want to accomplish with your day or your week. Keep that list handy too and check it off as you chip away at it.

Back to the present time, 2021: There's something about list making that's important. I make one every single day, even now, age 85. Every evening, while you're watching TV or just lazing around, take the time to make a list of the six or seven things you really want to do tomorrow. That way, you won't have to think about them during the night. And put the list where you see it first thing the next morning, so you can go to your computer or cell phone and check them off one at a time.

And wouldn't you like to be on someone's list of role models? Let's stop right now and make a toast, one that's worth repeating every evening and the next morning: "Here's to today and tomorrow. To hell with yesterday." I'll end this chapter with another smile line from George Burns -- "I can't die now — I'm booked."

Chapter Three

WHERE DID THE YEARS GO?

"Never ask old people how they are if you have anything else to do that day."

"DAMN--IT MAKES ME so mad." Mother stood before a hallway mirror gently massaging an arthritic hand. "What makes you mad, Mom?" I was looking at an attractive lady in her early seventies. "Old age. It's a pain in the neck in fact, it's a pain almost everywhere. On top of that, suddenly you look like someone's Grandmother, physically you don't bounce back, you don't recuperate quickly, and I never would have tolerated this pot belly on me when I was in my forties and fifties. Now, I say, who the hell cares."

Okay, let's use Mom's mirror observations as a guidepost to determine how we feel about aging. Do you have to accept old age as the ultimate punishment? Does it automatically mean that all your energies of your younger years are going to disappear? That you have no recourse but to lie down and let age wash over you like some crushing tidal wave? Is the mid-section going to become your spare tire? Do the age lines mean your face will never be again? Does the lack of hair mean, like Samson, you've lost your virility? Are you now someone who scouts should help across streets? Should your children become your parents now? Perhaps your employers would be smart to put you out to pasture to make room for some of the up-and-coming younger people on the staff!! Or as Robert Orben said, "Old people shouldn't eat health foods. They need all the preservatives they can get."

My oh my, don't you just love wallowing in self-pity? If that last paragraph is describing you, you may be in for a hard time with this book. I love people too much to let them hammer themselves up on an emotional cross. Don't think I'm going to be Pollyannaish about age. We all know the problem is very real and is not going to go away. But what you're going to learn to do is face up to it and win.

One of my nearest and dearest ageless friends commented, "I always thought I would grow older and grow in stature and importance, and finally become someone rather grand and important, you know, like Eleanor Roosevelt, or Angela Merkel, the Prime Minister of Germany. But of course, it wasn't true--I just grew older." But she (my friend) also realized that while not becoming an international star, she wasn't diminished by age either. She remained what she had always been--vital, interesting, full of life, and living every moment of her life without dwelling on a possibly hard future.

She said, "I know there might be some tough years ahead. Hopefully, I won't have a long, tedious illness, and I'm fortunate in that I don't have a financial problem--but I refuse to go out and buy some uninteresting condominium because it has nearby nursing care or is all on one floor, so I won't have a problem using my electric wheelchair when and if I need one. Besides, I'm too busy doing other interesting things every day to worry about all that other stuff."

Sunday Morning, February 10, 1985, St. Thomas, American Virgin Islands. (Remember I wrote this book 40+ years ago) I'm sitting in one of my favorite places in the world, on one of the covered patios that surround the home of my dear friends Honor and Carl Tranum. It's been two and a half years since Carl left this world. But every morning around 6:00 or 6:30 we'd sit out on this patio and enjoy our coffee and listen to the surf far below us on Magen's Bay, and the soft cooing of mourning doves drifting in and out of the lush, green jungle surrounding the house.

Carl and I spent many an hour with little conversation but always sharing our love of life and the camaraderie of close friendship. I love thinking about Carl and Honor--our friendship meant and means so much to me. In a few minutes, sweet Honor will appear, in shorts, tee-shirt and sneakers, and a Good Morning smile. She'll squeeze us some orange juice, we'll have a bowl of high fiber cereal, washed down with some high-energy conversation--and then we'll drive down the hill to Magen's Bay and she'll jog (I'll walk as she jogs) from one end of Magen's to the other--two miles total. She says it forces her to breathe deeper and certainly gets her heartbeat up. Honor is 75. Much of the day will be spent whipping up and down the steep hills of St. Thomas, Honor driving her four on the floor Mazda (left hand side of the road driving) and always discussing the newest and best in literature.

"One of the joys of being a senior citizen," says Honor, "is that for the first time in your life, you're not so busy raising a family and doing things for other people so you have time to read, I mean, really read, and be up to date on everything."

Let's stop for a moment and think about that. Perhaps you're thinking, well, Jim's friend isn't exactly poor, living down there in the islands. Right--she isn't poor. Her adoring husband, who often said she sure as hell didn't marry me for my money, made sure she would never have to worry about finances. And goodness knows, the one time in your life you shouldn't have to worry about money is when you're older. But even if you find yourself living on a very limited income, and don't have an over-flowing savings account (and we'll have some financial advice for you farther along in the book), your social security, and hopefully, some loving and grateful children will help now and then, so you don't have any major worries. But you'll also have more time to yourself than you've ever had before. You don't have to belong to all the book clubs to read all that's new.

Libraries don't charge. And unless you're a hermit, you should be very busy developing a support system, a network of friends, and between all of you, set up a lending and borrowing library. You're never lonely with a book. Okay, so much for the joys of reading. By the way, even if your eyesight is bad, there are big print publications, and big print editions of major newspapers, and now lots of "recorded books". I have one incredible friend who just now (I'm back in 2020) turned 101 years old, and *who is completely blind from macular degeneration, who says she's read everything.* She means, she's *heard* everything. You'd be amazed how good the recorded books are.

Don't be shy, tell the kids precisely what you want for your birthday or Christmas--a subscription to the large print New York Times, (or some other publication that isn't too politically biased) or three or four CD's or cassettes of your favorite books. And of course, a player for listening to those books. (And, back in the year of 2021, a Kindle is handy if your arthritis makes holding a book uncomfortable.) And I just discovered (in 2021) that I can ask ALEXA (buy one if you don't have one already) to READ any book I mention if it's in my Kindle library. Alexa has a nice voice.

Let's continue this general discussion of the many facets of aging. How about sex appeal--Surely the loss of that is harder on a woman than a man. If a woman suddenly finds men aren't innocently (or not innocently) flirting with her anymore, not smiling at her with appreciative glances, it can hurt. But it's how you handle the hurt that makes the difference.

You must expect some of your charms to be less magnetic. That's one of the realities of aging. Don't make a mistake and try to compensate for your perceived "lack". You know you don't like to see older women wearing too much makeup, or the hair dyed too blatant a color. Now I'm not advocating that you should just let everything go natural. That's silly. A little makeup carefully applied is a gentle reminder to the world that you are a woman and intend to go on looking like one. Hate that grey? Wash it away, or if you can afford it, have a professional beautician help color your hair in the most complimentary shade for your coloring. Find a fragrance that says You.

And of course, there's no excuse for having too much tummy. Keep your weight down. You'll look a thousand times better...and be healthier. Note: My mother, who at 72 had a pot belly, now at age 77, is a svelte size 8, and is looking better and dressing better than ever. Even if you don't feel strong enough to do hard exercise, a weight control diet plus gentle exercise (take a nice long walk every day or night) will keep you looking 100 times better.

Gents, do you feel left out in this discussion of sex appeal? You don't have makeup to hide the ills of aging, but you can do the rest of it. You can even tint your hair--or if you need it, if "bald" hurts, get a hairpiece. Why not? if it bothers you, do something about it. And certainly, you shouldn't have a big gut on you. Doesn't look nice. And pay close attention to your grooming. Clean, clean, clean, body and spirit and fingernails and teeth and smelling good. There's nothing sexier than clean.

Back to the present. I'm amazed that at my current 85 years, women often comment about a cologne I might be wearing, and I certainly don't put on much. I think they feel complimented that I still care enough about presenting the best possible version of myself to them. Hmmmm?

Who knows, even though the passion of passion itself may have passed you by, trust me when I tell you there is still a lot of joy in the companionship of another human being--a hand to hold, a soft embrace, someone to smile at on the other side of the table. And doctors say that you can actually go on enjoying sex into your 80's. What a nice thought. (I think. I mean, I wrote that when I was maybe 44, not 86, when I'm not positive how to spell Sechs. Or is it Seks.) Did you ever believe you could laugh at the memory of sex?

Mind you, anything goes in the pursuit of personal satisfaction and happiness. On a more serious vein, if you are too young to be having an impotence problem, and the virility pills aren't happening, they are having great success with penile implants. And ladies, just because surgery is surgery, I don't really recommend facelifts after age 65, but there's little or no pain involved with them--there is discomfort--but it may be worth it to lose 10 years off your face.

Think about it. Is there still more to discuss about age? Of course, there is. Age covers every subject and every emotion in the world. Basically, besides the physical stigma it can put on your body, the real burden of age is a state of mind. It's true--you are as old as you feel. And if you let yourself feel old, you will be old. You will limit your ability to live and to enjoy every single day on its own merits.

Right this moment I want you to sit back and think what absolutely bugs you most about being "older." Is it health? Sex appeal? Being retired from business? Loss of energy? Feeling unfulfilled? Think about it, get a firm fix in your head, and write it down, "I hate growing older because_____!" Okay, now try to *think* positively. For starters, you have more time to do everything you didn't do over the past thirty years.

What isn't bad about growing older? You're not working so damn hard. You have time to read. Give me enough food and enough books and I think I could spend maximum time on a deserted island. (Okay, I admit, I would still miss having a bidet.) Back to what isn't so bad about being, [I still hate to say the word] elderly: Time to smell the roses. Time to enjoy your children and/or grandchildren. Do you notice all the positive elements of aging revolve around time? I'll bet that when you and I finish going through this book together, that one of the big decisions you're going to have to make is how to make better use of your time.

Aging is a double-edged sword with time. In the long run, you may have less time left in terms of active life. On the other hand, with age, you have a gift of more everyday time. If you don't make use of that time, you're cheating yourself.

Now that you have the time to think about what you never had enough time to do, I want you to write it down. At last, I have enough time today, to _____. Okay, what did you write? Read? Write letters? Take painting lessons? Help the church? Really get to know your grandchildren. Counsel troubled people? Garden? Study Italian, or cooking? Learn how to swim? Learn needlepoint? Really be a good Democrat…or Republican? Eliminate all your poor health and physical habits? (Everyone should take the time to do that—every day!)

Since we now have the time, let's take some to target in on some of what could be bad habits which have surfaced along with age. It's easy to become set in your ways. George Bernard Shaw said (and I will quote him often because he was so brilliant): "We don't stop playing because we grow old; we grow old because we stop playing."

Are you getting like that? Now let's not just shrug that off—think about it. It's a very common "older" attitude. Suddenly, without realizing it, you've lost much of your flexibility toward people, things, events. You want what you want, and you want it right now—and you want it according to your rules.

Sorry, you don't call all the shots. You can't always have your way—so there. If you're using your age as an emotional crutch to beat people over the head, stop it. Let's take another meaningful thought from Bernard Shaw (he didn't use the George): "A life spent making mistakes is not only more honorable, but more useful than a life spent doing nothing."

So, what to do about this attitude? I want you to realize that most of the things that you get all puffed up about are totally unimportant. Who cares if your daughter doesn't clean the kitchen exactly as you clean it —at least she cleans it. Who cares if people drive dopey —it's just a reminder for you to drive more carefully and to keep your eyes on the road at all times. Especially in this era of cell phones!

Who cares if your grandchildren don't write thank-you letters right away? If you think your children aren't teaching their children proper manners, and it really bugs you, either write a brief note to the parents or the kid. Pick your words carefully. Some children are too thin-skinned to have Mama tell them how to raise their children. If that's the case, don't write in anger (in fact try not to do anything in anger), write a love note. Example. "I love Billy so much I'd like to give him a thump on the head for not writing a proper thank you note. I guess kids these days are so busy with their cell phones and Social Media they forget some of the little niceties of life." Then you can twit, text or email Billy: "I suppose the shirt I sent you didn't fit properly, so you gave it to your pet baboon who will no doubt write me a thank-you letter soon. Do give him my email address." Well of course Billy won't expect that kind of note from his Granny...all the better reason to send it. Remember —you may have lived several years, but you aren't *old*. You still have a sense of humor. You are still someone to reckon with, to love, to enjoy, and to write thank-you letters to.

Guess what? Today and tomorrow are more important than all the yesterday's in the world. What am I getting at? Just reminding you to stop living in the past. Don't grow old because you've stopped playing.

It's fine to remember the past, to think lovingly of that man or woman you wish had lived forever... but make the memory a positive thought, rather than a sad recollection. Remember the good and the silly and the loving and try to incorporate some of those attitudes in your daily actions. You still can be good and silly and loving. Keeping all those facets in your personality are what will make you a sparkling person to be with, not just another "senior citizen". Life isn't about finding yourself. Life is about creating yourself.

A momentary comment on the term, senior citizen. I think a more satisfying term might be Elder Statesman/Woman, or perhaps AdultPlus. Maybe we'll create a word, Peterson. Okay, I guess I can live with Senior Citizen, or even Elder, but I'd rather not be called "The Old Guy".

Let's find another bad habit and deal with it. Do you sit around and complain? Poor me. Eliza on the ice growing old and all alone. Well, if that's you—stop it right now. How boring, how unproductive, what a waste of your time and everyone else's. Anyone who sits around wrapping themselves in veils of self-pity is going to deserve everything they get. And what they'll get is "aloneness". If that's what you're going to do, you might as well go out and sit on a sidewalk somewhere with a sign, TAKE PITY ON ME, and a hat where passersby can throw coins at you. Boooorrrring!

Mind you, I'm not whitewashing the aging process. It's all right to get a little angry because you're growing older and not liking it, if the anger doesn't take over. Anger can be a good stimulus for getting off your duff and doing something with yourself, but the minute you feel the anger turn you into a hopeless living organism, a mass of blood vessels and cartilage waiting for someone to pull the plug on you, you're losing the battle. That's when you stand up and give yourself a hard lecture about the evils of self-pity and the destructiveness of excessive anger. Remind yourself at those bad times about all the delicious time you have now and ask yourself what you are doing with it and go out and do something worthwhile.

Maybe that something is just reading a book, or perhaps it's more active… like picking up a paint brush and taking a shot at art or taking a lesson in something. Another choice? Go help someone who's really in awful shape. If nothing else comes to mind, clean out your closet or dresser drawers. Isn't that always satisfying? I find myself, when being non-productive, taking on a cleaning task because it makes me feel so much better when I'm finished.

I'm going to interrupt my story or advice or whatever you want to call it, with some terrific, *admirable thinking from an Admiral. Admiral William H. McRaven* gave a commencement address to the graduating class of the University of Austin. And it's wonderful, wise and an internal reminder to all of us. He titled his speech: MAKE YOUR BED. In it, Admiral McRaven shares the ten lessons he learned from Navy SEAL training. Here they are, and all of us should take them to heart:

1. Start your day with a task completed (i.e., make your bed. I do, first thing when I get up in the morning).

2. You can't go it alone. (Like row a boat.)

3. Only the size of your heart matters.

4. Life's not fair — drive on!

5. Failure can make you stronger.

6. You must dare greatly.

7. Stand up to the bullies.

8. Rise to the occasion.

9. Give people hope.

10. Never, ever quit!

Aren't those great thinking points? No, I'll correct that — not just thinking points — great action points. You might like his easy-to-read book, "Make Your Bed."

When you feel you've come to the end of your rope, always give yourself some space for thinking out your problems. Get out of the house. Take a walk. At least you'll be exercising and therefore doing something good for yourself. You'll also see things differently and be able to clear your head and your thoughts and come to a reasonable solution. If you're stuck inside, pacing isn't bad either, but it's even nicer if weather and neighborhood (and hour of the day or night) allow you to go outside and commune with a Higher Power—and yourself.

Speaking of that Higher Power, whoever He/She or It is (don't get nervous, I'm not only a believer, but I'm also a Ruling Elder in my congregation), God is a good person to talk to. It doesn't mean you have to become a "born again" Christian, but it really isn't necessary. Praying is a quiet, deeply personal experience. Whether you do it in church or in the privacy of your own bedroom, it can be very satisfying to talk things over with God. You may not always get some divine revelation, but then again, you just might. Or perhaps the revelation will come from within because you'll be listening to yourself for a change. Try praying out loud. I do. Guess I want to make sure he hears me. And cross my fingers and hope to...no, not die, but hope to go on praying, because I feel certain He's up there listening. And speaking about praying out loud. . .

I remember giving myself a lecture, 58 years ago. Before seeing my new baby daughter, I was waiting outside a Brooklyn Hospital, all alone, speaking out loud, smoking one of my two packs of Marlboro's a day, and I said (mind you, this was the year BEFORE they announced smoking causes cancer), *Why are you doing this, Jim? You don't have a strong throat and always have a long-lasting sore throat every winter, and you know these things must be bad for you and you know you don't want either of your baby daughters to ever smoke*, and I stomped the cigarette out and NEVER smoked again! That's why I'm still here at 85, writing this love note/memoir to you. Since it makes me smile to share

George Bernard Shaw's thoughts with you, he had a perfect one for smoking: "A cigarette is a pinch of tobacco rolled in paper with fire at one end and a fool at the other."

I'd like to end this chapter with a quote from a fine author you'll meet later, Malcolm Cowley. The quote is from his wise and wonderful book, "The View From 80," in which he quotes John Cowper Powys's book "The Art of Growing Old, published when Mr. Powys was 72, although he lived to age 90. He said, "The one supreme advantage that Old Age possesses over Middle Age and Youth is its nearness to Death. The very thing that makes it seem pitiable to those less threatened and therefore less enlightened, is the thing that deepens, heightens, and thickens out its felicity." He also said, "We poor dullards of habit and custom, we besotted and befuddled takers of life for granted, require the hell of a flaming thunderbolt to rouse us to the fact that every single second of conscious life is a miracle past reckoning, a marvel past all computation."

Read it again. There are a lot of good thoughts in this chapter you can incorporate. But for now, let's push on, and open another door.

Chapter Four

MEET SOME OF MY DEAR OLD FRIENDS, SOME OF WHOM ARE FAMOUS, ALL ARE MEMORABLE

"It takes about ten years to get used to how old you are." — Unknown

"*I* *FEARED THE WORST, the numb, hard-to-find pain that was somewhere in my shoulders had moved down my arm. Now it felt as though all the muscle fiber had been sucked out by syringes. There was a weakness there, and a pain, especially if I raised my arm at all. I had had other symptoms in the past which hadn't panned out into anything, but now I knew — this was it. If it wasn't bursitis, it was something worse, and age would finally take its final toll on me. Perhaps I* *would be crippled and unable to write or do anything. I suffered a million pains and worried about the future I surely wouldn't have. Can you imagine such BS? That was me. Every gas attack was stomach cancer, every headache a tumor. No, I hadn't been a hypochondriac—this was just my reaction to aging, to being retired. I remember thinking what a sarcastic bastard my doctor was when he greeted me on one visit with "Well, what is it this week, Gordon?" In the long run, it was my Helen, wife of 37 years who said, using the old but still good for a laugh line, "I married you for better and for worse but not for lunch." But then she added, "And I'm a lousy nurse, so what are you doing with the rest of your life anyway—is it just going to be a series of strange undiagnosable illnesses?"*

"It sunk in, and I gave myself a long, serious lecture, and decided that I had been acting the fool. And mind you this was over a period of about two years. I pronounced myself well and rejoined humanity, and it was amazing how much strength I still had. I even took some freelance jobs (at the insistence of a younger, wiser friend) and felt like myself again. Now, 7 years after deciding I was dying of everything, I'm looking forward to, oh, I don't know, I'm looking forward to living every day. Hopefully there be lots of them, but I will not worry about it."

I know Gordon and he's a charming man—78 years young. He and his beloved Helen still take wonderful vacations and he is still a handsome guy, appealing and funny and interesting. *(Side note: Gordon lived to a productive 87 years of age, still producing up to the very end of his wonderfully satisfying life.)* Stop for a moment and think of yourself. Are you "thinking yourself" into an early grave? Aches and pains aren't unusual with age, 99% of them are just part of the aging process. Many of them will disappear or are only temporary interruptions in a normally active life.

(This is all from the original manuscript in 1977/78) Let's say goodbye to Gordon so I can introduce you to a wildly wonderful couple. Mildred Gilman and her husband Bob Wohlfarth came to my country inn one day for lunch, to visit my/their good friend, Honor Tranum. It seems Mildred and Bob had lived in Troutbeck (the inn) when it was a private home. In 1930, Honor's father (remember, Troutbeck had been her family home) had given the Wolfarth's a year at his expense, to write and create anything of their choosing. Oh, wouldn't any of us love a gift like that.

They both wrote a book, and hers was sold to the movies for a whopping $10,000. (Wow, that was really Big money back in the 30's!) You see Mildred had been a "sob-sister". That's what they called women reporters during those days of yellow journalism and Mildred's book was naturally titled, "Sob-Sister". Her stories of being a Hearst reporter, of using the first telephone from a plane, of submarine trips, of being on a gangster's hit list, were all colorful and charming. At the time of our meeting, she was working on an auto- biography. "She's soft-pedaled the whole thing," said her husband Bob..."she's a wimp." "I am not a wimp--I'm just trying to protect our oldest child's image of his mother." "Hah", said Bob. "What image. She's just pulling her punches." "Younger men are so idealistic" countered the unstoppable Mildred. She was 89. And Bob was a young guy, just 82.

There she was, stylish slacks, comfortable but sharp looking shoes, a sweater over the slacks, belted on the outside. She sparkled. The smile flashed an easy openness. The eyes were bright and alert. And every day she arose to do 100 stretching exercises, then followed that with a three-mile bike ride (not the stationary kind) through the countryside. Daytimes found her either at her typewriter (not easy believe me) or elbow deep in dirt, doing her gardening.

I think one of the things I enjoyed most about the ebullient Mildred is that she and the natty Bob (I should look that good when I'm 60, let alone 82) went down to their kitchen every morning where a large sign was posted--"Defend Yourself". But more than the humor of the sign, what I really loved is that Mildred doesn't have an elderly mindset. She isn't going to stop living tomorrow or next week or next year or probably not in the next ten years. She's living now. Her age, if anything, is an encouragement to not wasting time. She makes use of it. And it's wonderful to see. I thank you Mildred and Bob (he still goes to the office in his publishing company at least twice a week) for giving us all something to work for. I know when you left Troutbeck that day, Honor said, "Mildred gives me hope—I'd like to think I can be that terrific when I'm 89." And of course, she will be.

Let's go back for a minute to the good Admiral's superb speech. He's not preaching a new faith, just reminding you to have some discipline and rules about your own life. Trust me, the simple act of making your bed can give you the lift you need to start your day right and put you on the path to end it right. He also wisely advises that if you want to change the world, find someone to help you paddle. You know you can't paddle the boat alone, even on a waveless lake. Find someone to share your life with. Make as many friends as possible, and never forget that your success depends on others.

"It's such a bloody bore." The speaker was my near and dear friend, Ruth West. "My eyes are getting so bad I don't even enjoy theatre anymore--at least visually. And I worry about taking a crosstown bus—first, that I'll trip getting on and off, and second, that I'll miss my stop because I just plain don't see things very well." You'd have to know Ruth to understand that at 84 she is ageless—I'd guess she's about 40, with a devastating wit and the brightest mind imaginable. We still spend a lot of time together, both of us pretending that the physical frailties aren't there. Because in truth, when you're with friends, they aren't.

Let's stick with Ruth, because she faced a tough decision and I want you to see how she faced it, head on, and took productive action. Realizing the problem with her eyes, and an inner ear issue affecting her balance, were not going to go away, Ruth researched and found a Ladies Home where she could admit herself. She would have a compact, three-room studio apartment in the building, with elevators of course, and the home is attached to a clinic where there's fulltime medical care if necessary. She laughingly said, "They've got to have some other old girls there just as bored as I am with being physically limited but are willing to play bridge or badmouth anyone we can specifically remember. Maybe together we can make some happy happen."

Ruth my love—you create happiness wherever you are. I cherish our friendship and am anticipating many more years of the same. (*Interesting, looking back to then. 40 years ago, we thought anyone who was 80 was a miracle if they were still walking. Nowadays—more than ever I want you to read and understand what I'm telling you—80 is not a miracle! I have lots of friends in their 80's—including myself, and I'm a friend to many—wondering if I'm still going to be "with it" five years from now when I'm 90????)*

For most of my adult life I've been in love with a wonderful man named Roger Hackney. Roger is my uncle, now deceased many years. Married more than 50 years to Margaret Flaherty Hackney, my father's sister, Roger is what all of us guys want to be when we grow up. Although his parents had lots of bucks (they owned Kansas or something like that), the story goes that they gave him a train ticket to New York, $25, and wished him well. Now, how true all that is I don't know and frankly I don't care, because it makes a good story. At any rate, Rog came to New York, and conquered it. He became very important and successful. Fortune Magazine, besides publishing his full-page portrait photo, once wrote him up as one of America's 50 best executives. He was Errol Flynnish handsome, rather rakish looking, with a gentle Great Plains manner and a mind like a stainless steel beartrap.

Besides the business success, life brought Peg and Roger two beautiful daughters, my cousins Ann and Cindy. The kids grew up in a stately home in Larchmont, New York. Roger continued to grow in business stature, handling a major international job with his customary ease. It seemed impossible back then: He would be in Belgium on Tuesday, Paris on Wednesday, San Francisco on Thursday.

Back about 55 years ago, let's see now, Roger would have been just 63 then, (I was 31) I moved my family to Larchmont. Though not quite as stately as my relative's home, we loved ours, and loved the town as a growing up place for the two Flaherty daughters. But I loved something else about Larchmont. It put me within easy reach of Uncle Roger.

Usually Sunday afternoon was our time. We'd sit and talk about everything under the sun for two to four hours at a stretch. I find it hard to believe that I could have been interesting enough to keep Roger fascinated all those hours. On the other hand, *maybe I was that interesting*? Maybe everyone was to Roger. You see, Roger had a great talent. *He listened. And I mean really listened.* When you talked to Roger, he heard what you said, he understood it, and probably learned something from you, and then, if prompted, would embellish your thoughts with his wisdom.

As Roger entered his 80s, he had some serious eye problems, but other than that, nothing changed. He still listened. And of course, he talked a lot too. And it was always interesting, always illuminating. He had a few comments about age that I want to share with you.

First, he talked about a new category of age, "Old Old," which is for people over 80. Mind you, he's talking about an attitude people had maybe 30 years ago. He said, *"It's hilarious. You must have a sense of humor to put up with some of the treatment you get at this age. People are so damn scared you're going to drop dead at their feet they "over care" for you. That's not to sound unappreciative for their concern, but it gets funny. I went out to the coast the other day to face a battery of lawyers for about 8 hours. After about 45 minutes of questioning, the attorney said, 'It's been almost one hour, Mr. Hackney, shouldn't we stop and rest now? Are you tired?' No, I replied, Why—are you?*

"To tell the truth, I don't accept emotionally the thought that I may die soon ...or ever. Obviously, I logically and intellectually accept the fact that I will not live forever. But I sure as hell am not going to die tomorrow or next week or next year unless something goes wrong with the basic machine." Aunt Peg, who for years has been cheerfully telling me she's on the way out, said something to the effect that Roger is living proof only the good die young. Peg, who continues to say she's had it and is over the hill, is an ageless 81, with a wicked sense of humor and a contemporary mindset. To you both, my sweet Aunt and Uncle, a loving hug from your nephew. You were always a source of

pleasure to me as well as a meaningful symbol of "family ties".

(This section was written maybe 43 years ago):"As you become older, art and life become the same thing." Artist George Brock said that. The quotation comes from a beautiful series of radio programs called *I'm Too Busy to Talk Now: Conversations with American Artists Over 70*, created by wonderful Connie Goldman, a talented and loving woman who conceived and produced the series. Connie is allowing me to share some of the wisdom of her American artists with you. Let's start with some comments from John Huston, the wonderful filmmaker--African Queen, Night of the Iguana, The Maltese Falcon, Under the Volcano, and most recently the critically acclaimed Prizzi's Honor, in which he directed his daughter and her lover/co-star, Jack Nicholson. He's 78 now, five marriages, five homes later, a writer, painter, actor, director-even gambler he says.

When asked about age. John Huston said the only change is physiological. "Now, if I have to climb steps I must stop and get my breath. I'm like a broken-down racehorse." Mr. Huston has emphysema, so breathing became a major problem in his life. "I had to stop smoking. I miss it but don't crave it." Did he anticipate old age? "No, it came to me as quite a shock. "I wasn't prepared for some of these revelations. I took to falling off horses, for example. These were sad recognitions. I find things excruciatingly funny. It comes from my father. I never laughed as hard with anyone as I did with my father." John doesn't see life as having time periods, like middle age. "It's all one thing … it's something called life.

"What is ludicrous is trying to stay young in-spite-of the evidence of age. It's sad. Aging flesh has its own beauty. I suggest they look at some Rembrandts." He has considered himself so physically and mentally healthy he's never had to think much about himself. To the question, "to what do you owe your longevity?" he answered: "Surgery •••and remembering to duck." (I don't know who said that first—John Huston or President Reagan.)

Huston attributes much of his peacefulness to the serenity of his surroundings. He lives in Mexico, in a jungle where "gossiping parrots settle in the morning, and you throw a seed in the ground and jump back." Huston had a favorite Bernard Shaw quote, too: "People who say it cannot be done should not interrupt those who are doing it."

Jessica Tandy and Hume Cronin are brilliant examples of American theatrical personalities who have lived many years and are still living, still performing, still creating. Hume Cronin said: "I don't want to end up with a smooth face, Let the lines get deeper, especially the laugh lines." Separately and together the two of them have won every award there is. Anyone who ever saw the two of them on stage, in The Fourposter, The Gin Game, and Foxfire, would understand why.

In 1969 I discovered a malignancy and lost an eye," said Cronin. "No big deal. I have fears and anxieties which turn into anger in me. I don't see as well anymore. Don't hear as well. It infuriates me that I don't do things as well as I used to." Jessica interrupted: "Yes you can. Oh, if anyone had said to me, when I started, this will be your position in life, that of a 75-year-old, I would have thought, Wow! How marvelous! But that was when no one, or not many, lived that long. Now we're able to keep active longer. You just keep doing. It's flexing your muscles.

"It's fine to vegetate for a bit between projects, but I love to go back to work." "The big difference," Hume said, "is that now we're choosier. We don't take any job that comes along. We just do what we want to do." "Being busy just for the sake of being busy is very nonproductive," said Jessica. "Even running a home well, making it a welcoming place, is a productive job."

"One should look ahead, learning from our past projects." Hume said, "Do you understand me more now"? She answered, "Never. You're an enigma, a lovely enigma."

He explained that there are so many abrasions to daily life--planning, arranging, handling all the nitty-gritty--that it's sometimes difficult to find the real time you need for yourself--time to be creative. And for the creative process to work, there must be enough rest. And you must be careful to get what you really like, or you will be forced to like what you get.

He said, "When you have someone to share the problems and joys with, the problems are cut in half and the joys are doubled." "I agree", Jessica said, "When the difficulties come, they can strengthen your relationship. And let's not forget that laughter is essential--even over the serious things. You'll be in trouble unless you can have a good time and laugh and find things, even the painful difficult things, funny too. One scene we were playing had sexual connotations the audience thought was very funny—but the author didn't! He didn't write it for humor and didn't understand their reaction. We couldn't stop laughing."

Hugh said, "Remember Samuel Becketts's famous line, *I can't go on, I can't go on...I'll go on.*" Jessica said, "it's a myth that people fall apart with age. That's a function of the individual. If you say you're over the hill, then you're over the hill..." Hugh quoted someone named Izzy Stone, who said, "I hope to die young—as late as possible." "You just hope you'll fight off this inevitable process of deterioration. So, keep swinging. Keep going with interests outside of yourself, and you won't think of all the aches. Shakespeare said it: "With mirth and laughter let all wrinkles come." Mr. Cronin and Ms. Tandy are starring in this year's movie hit, Cocoon!

Balladeer Burl Ives says, "When I look at the mirror, there's a moment of hilarity ... is that old coot with the funny look in his eye, me?" Burl Ives is aging with gentle humor. "Material things at this point begin to diminish in your life. There's no end to development and creativity--it's all part of the process of living." Burl is 76 now but hasn't closed shop. He lives a little quieter these days, in the mountains outside of Santa Barbara, California. "The mind controls the whole business. If your mind says I'm old and crippled, you are. But if your mind says I will not give in to my ailments, they will go away. Guess what—they will, and they will be replaced by new energies."

How do you cope with the changes in your body? "Every morning I spend two hours, while still in bed, working on my voice. So, I'm singing better than ever. My voice is improving. Yes, the body gets older, but the person gets smarter. I know I can't do the things I used to do. You must adjust. I rarely drink these days. I'm happier now, have more fun now." Mr. Ives said, "In my younger days I was ambitious. Now I never go out. I'd rather eat here. When I was younger, went out all the time—no social calendar—just work.

"Whitman wrote: There was a child that went forth one day—and what that child saw—he became. That was true of me, too. I was a sponge. I soaked up everything. Dorothy, my wife, and I, were walking on the same path, so I just took her hand and we walked together. I couldn't believe the intimacy of that moment. Try it, you'll see. Another important part of my life should be true for everyone. I feel no different than I did 20 years ago. I know I am different. But I'm not aware of it.

"I always like the story of Tom Payne, when chided by someone for his age, said something like: The house that Tom Payne has some problems—the roof leaks, it's cold in winter, and doesn't run really well—but that's just the house that Tom Payne lives in, there's nothing wrong with Tom Payne."

After you read this book, there's another, little book I mentioned earlier that you absolutely must read if you haven't already. It will also give you the opportunity of knowing a positively delightful human being. Malcolm Cowley has been a gifted writer all his life. Now, in his 80s, he has brought us another gift, a small, easy-to-read book, I mentioned earlier: "The View From 80". Written for Life Magazine in 1978, it was so popular they persuaded him to expand the article a little into this most charming peek into the private world of the elderly.

Taking nothing from his slender and beguiling piece of literature, let me list some messages the body and its surroundings have for you when it wants to tell you, You Are Old:

1. When it becomes an achievement to do thoughtfully, step by step, what you once did instinctively.

2. When your bones ache.

3. When there are more and more little bottles in the cabinet, with instructions for taking four times a day.

4. When you fumble and drop your toothbrush (butterfingers).

5. When your face has bumps and wrinkles so that you cut yourself while shaving (blood on the towel).

6. When year by year your feet seem farther from your hands.

7. When you can't stand on one leg and have trouble pulling on your pants.

8. When you hesitate on the landing before walking down a flight of stairs.

9. When you spend more time looking for things you misplaced than you spend using them after you (or usually your wife) has found them.

10. When you fall asleep in the afternoon.

11. When it becomes harder to remember two things at once.

12. When a pretty girl passes you in the street and you don't turn your head.

13. When you forget names, even of people you saw last month (the poet Conrad Aiken said at 80, "Names? I'm starting to forget Nouns".)

14. When you listen hard to jokes and catch everything but the snapper.

15. When you decide not to drive at night anymore.

16. When everything takes longer to do—bathing, shaving, getting dressed or undressed—but time passes quickly, as if you were gathering speed while coasting downhill. The year from 79 to 80 is like a week when you were a boy.

I want all of you to promise me you'll run out and try to buy a copy of The View From 80, or if you have no luck buying it, go to your public library. It's a must read if you want to graduate from my course. Thank you, Mr. Cowley for your wonderful point of view. You taught me some things I needed to know.

You probably have tales to tell as well. Maybe they're not as famous as some of the not-so-famous and famous people you've met on the preceding pages. So, tell me. Share your wisdom with me, and I'll share it with all our Dear Old Friends here and abroad.

Let's end with another perfect thought from the brilliant G. Bernard Shaw: "The person I miss most is the one I could have been."

And there is humor, well, maybe black humor, but humor in Getting Old. Here are some funnies I've recently come across. Come on, admit it, some of these make you smile:

• You drop something. When you were younger you just pick it up. When you're older and you drop something, you stare at it for a bit contemplating if you actually need it anymore."

• When you're dead, you don't know you're dead. Only others feel the pain. The same thing happens when you're stupid."

• One way to find out if you are old is to fall in front of a lot of people. If they laugh, you're still young. If they panic and start running to you, you're old."

• Try to remember the greener grass across the fence may be due to a septic tank."

• I've found that growing up in the sixties was a lot more fun than being in my sixties."

- And just like that 1971 was 50 years ago."

- If your eyes hurt after you drink coffee, you have to take the spoon out of the cup."

- I find, these days, that most of my conversations start out with: Did I tell you this already? Or What was I going to say?

- I never wish death upon anybody who wrongs me. I wish sudden explosive diarrhea while on a date, with frequent sneezes."

- You never appreciate what you have till it's gone. Toilet paper is a good example.

- The best part about getting old is ... Nothing. Getting Older Sucks."

Bless Bob Hope for all the smiles he gave us: On turning 90: "You know you're getting old when the candles cost more than the cake." They asked him where he wanted to be buried, Bob replied: "Surprise me." When he hit 100, "I don't feel old. In fact, I don't feel anything until noon. Then it's time for my nap."

A Japanese couple is arguing about how to perform highly erotic sex:

------ Husband: *"Sukitaki. Mojitaka!"*
------ Wife Replies: *"Kowanini! Mowi janakpa!"*

------ Husband angrily says: *"Toka a anji roki roumi yakoo!"*

------ Wife, on her knees, begging: *"Mimi Nakoundinda tinkouji!"*

------ Husband shouts angrily: *"Na miaou kina Tim kouji.!"*

My goodness, friends, I can't believe you just sat there trying to read this! You don't know any Japanese! You'll read anything if it's about sex...sometimes I worry about you. I laugh at all of these, knowing they're all kind of true. And you know the (Old) person I laughed with most of all?

My one-of-a-kind, super-terrific, intelligent, beautiful, loving, kind and wisely demanding Mother. And now, you get to meet her up close.

Chapter Five

Mom and me

"Grab it while you can—grab every scrap of happiness while you can." Noel Coward

I WANT A GIRL just like the girl that married dear old dad. Not totally true. I don't think one should want to marry one's mother. What you should want is a mother like mine. Meet Mary White Flaherty Zabriskie. She was born in Centralia, Illinois, April 9, 1909. She is one terrific dame. And I want to put in print that I have been incredibly fortunate to have this excellent woman around to help guide me through the pitfalls (and pedestals) of life.

I remember when I was a little boy, like age 6 to 10, mothers came to school a lot in those days, and I would think, "My mother is prettier than the other mothers." And she was. She never threw on a house dress and bedroom slippers. She would put on adequate makeup, comb her hair and dress perfectly. She was, after all (she told me this in later years) Jim Flaherty's wife, and she had to look right. Dad was the District Attorney back in the 40s.

I'm hazy about much of my childhood. I know it was happy and good and all the right things, but when my father died in my 14th year, I blocked out many of the childhood memories. A psychiatrist friend said not to worry, I didn't have to remember everything. It had all been so happy and satisfying there were no hidden traumas waiting to drag me into some black depths of depression. But from the time my father died, there was just mom (I always called her "mother" just as one of my daughters always calls me "father") and me. Like a pair of mixed cymbals, we would have a quick, silly battle every morning when she would cheerfully sing (knowing it bugged me), "schoolboy, schoolboy, time to get up, time to get up".

Let me back up for a minute. When my father, a very prominent attorney in the Miami area, died, I was understandably devastated. And when I got home after church (he had died on a Sunday morning), Mother was there with her best friends gathered around and she said, "now it's just the two of us, so you'll have to be my good strong right arm." Mind you, this was before Jackie Kennedy brought dignity to death in front of the cameras of the world.

We went through the sad rosary service, everyone weeping in mother's face, and she comforted each one of them, thanking them. When we reached the over-flowing cathedral for the funeral itself, I remember her taking my arm and whispering, "Stand straight the way your father likes it." If occasionally a tear escaped (she was only 41) there was never some disturbing public show of emotion. She told me in later years, "I was a textbook hysteric case in the privacy of my bedroom, screaming at God, Why Me, Why Me •••I wanted to hit my head against the wall. Thank goodness I had you and that was the best reason for me to get hold of myself and get off my cross and get on with life."

If you're thinking what this story of a 41-year-old widow has to do with aging gracefully, just stick with me, you'll see.

It's important to understand you are at 50 what you are at 25. And just as you have known boring OLD people in their 30s, don't think for a minute they are suddenly going to become fascinating sages as they age? Do you? Believe you me, it doesn't happen. Old at 30 is older at 60.

But here comes the good part. If you know you were always fun and slightly crazy in the good sense of that word as a young adult, why the hell should you change now? Do you think because you're now in your 70s that you are no longer fun? That your conversation no longer sparkles? That you no longer brighten a room with your personality when you enter? Stop thinking that way. You are still you. Maybe the skin isn't as tight. The hair isn't as shiny. But you've earned those laugh lines. And God knows you know a whole lot more than you did way back then. If anything, chances are you're even more fascinating than you were back in your "young" prime. Now you're in a different kind of prime, but don't for a minute discount it. Mom didn't. When she was in her 70s and 80s and would come North to visit me, my friends (in their 40s and 50s) would compete to sit next to Mary at dinner parties.

And although I certainly recognize the importance and comforting aspect of having buddies your own age, don't think that a friendly 45-year-old or 32-year-old is "just being nice" to an old timer. Chances are he or she is thrilled to have a friend as accomplished, as smooth, as winning, as charming, as terrific as you. Personally, I can tell you some of my happiest days were spent arm and arm with loving friends in their 70's and 80's. Yes, perhaps I was a little more protective of them than with chums from my same generation. But what's wrong with that?

Gorillas Hum When They Eat Their Favorite Food. Aren't you glad I told you? Hell's bells, it's nicer to think about than Pandemics and new, more contagious variants of the hideous virus and street protests and the rise of violent crime in the cities. Huh? Is all that ugly really happening? I'm writing this in March 2021. I just this morning got my first vaccination. Also just found a good note reminding us of things we'll never take for granted after this virus is just an ugly memory: A handshake with a stranger; Conversations or a last-minute supper with neighbors; A crowded theater; Friday night out; Taste of communion; A routine checkup; The school rush each morning; Coffee with a friend; The stadium roaring; Each deep breath; A boring Tuesday. All true, hmmm?

Are you old enough to remember when life kind of had a plan? You would get through grade and high school and go (hopefully) away to college and graduate and Get a Job, and maybe meet the boy-or-girl of your dreams and imagine the babies you would make and get married.

It wasn't impossible. I graduated from Michigan State in 1957 (the Vice-President of the United States, Richard

Nixon, gave the commencement address). I went there because back in the mid-50s, ONLY two schools in America offered a degree in Communications. My darling mother came to see me graduate. And then we drove to New York in my 10-year-old Oldsmobile. It was the first car I ever owned. I bought it for $100 in East Lansing, Michigan. Sold it for $50 in NYC.

There was a recession in NYC that year, but I finally got a job! Allied Stores hired me as an Executive Trainee in Sales Promotion. Sounded reasonably important. I was paid $3,400—that was a full year's salary. Imagine, after taxes, I took home only $200 A MONTH, and was living in New York City, with no money from home, not because my Mom and Stepfather were cheap, there just was no money. Maybe I'm justifying the memory, but I don't think it hurt me to be poor—and survive. In truth, I don't remember feeling poor—I just didn't have any money. And my first tacky walkup fifth floor apartment had a drunk superintendent, so it was rare to have hot water. But I had an uncle not too far away and he let me use his shower a few nights every week. I was drunk too—with the glamor of WORKING. I swear to you right now, even way back then, earning next to nothing, I woke up every morning, thrilled to be able to go to work and learn something, and maybe do something that would make me stand out from the crowd. *Funny? Not really, I was just a budding work-aholic, a condition I have loved my entire life.*

Okay, think along with me. Would I have been better off with some family money, maybe even living in Mom and Dad's (non-existent) palatial apartment on upper Fifth Avenue with a private chef serving the evening meal, hmmm? Would that have made me a better person than I am now? Doubtful.

But now I'm 86 and there are some investments and some cash (not tons, but enough to feel reasonably secure) in the bank, AND (God must have decided I was an okay guy) my life is brightened by a Nanny who lives full time with me and makes sure my home is shiny, the dogs smiling, and delicious food is on the table. But because the stocks, money and Nanny weren't always there, I still make my bed every morning, and if there's a dish in the sink, I wash it and still have no qualms about questioning bills from suppliers.

But I won't question giving some money to someone who's health or career has thrown them between that proverbial but very real rock and a hard place. I talked to a girl, well, she was over 40, on TWINE one day, and if you don't know what TWINE is, find out. They put you in touch with someone you don't know at all, and almost never lives near you, usually across the country, and you have 15 minutes---yeah, 15 minutes to establish a connection, to talk about something that's meaningful.

It's a great service for lonely people. I'm not lonely, but I admire what they do, so I became a TWINE partner, . . . and I know I'm rambling.

Anyway, this one nice gal was stuck in one of the cities we've grown to pity, i.e., Seattle or Portland, and wanted to get out, but couldn't earn enough in that metropolitan mess, and she was saving to put $1,000 together to return to Texas where she had a best friend to live with and could certainly get a job more in keeping with her experience and intelligence.

I didn't say anything to her but asked for her address so I could send her one of my novels, which I did--but I also sent her a check for a thousand dollars. I told her it wasn't a loan. It was an investment on my part. I was buying a share of her future, so she wouldn't become a tax burden or a personal pain to family and friends. I told her to not worry about paying it back. And I didn't expect some tear-stained thank you card. Maybe someday, a quick note, like: "Life's good, Jim. I'm looking forward to tomorrow, and all the tomorrows after that." Thanks. S------." And you know something! Four months later I got that note, a happy one, with her check for $1,000. I sent the check back to her, and said something smart-alecky like, "You dummy, you already paid me—with 100% interest on my investment." Talk about feeling good about yourself. Hmm, in reading this right now wonder if I did that just to feel better about myself?

Am I always that good, that giving, that generous and caring? Naw. Although, I try. My nature, shaped by my glorious Mother, was to live by the Golden Rule, *Do unto others as you would have others do unto you.* Early on, I decided the thought was wonderful, but the combination of words was awkward, so I rewrote it: **You Get What You Give.** And I always gave Nice, and Friendly, and Generous and Helpful. But in these later years, faced with the heaviest emotional burden of my life, care-giving, and caretaking my partner of 48+ years, who had, with no warning, slipped into Dementia plus four times a day Dialysis, found myself wondering if I can stay patient, keep on smiling, keep on giving? Good ole approachable Jim began to doubt the depths of his ability to give. But I got through it, even though every day was a challenge, and many were painful. He died June 15, 2021. Here's to his immeasurable talent.

The truth? I'm impatient with mediocre thinking, or more often than mediocre, just people's incapability to do certain things, to respond certain ways. This impatience with others has made me stop and think long and hard about who I was and who I am capable of being. I repeat (to myself) a friend's comment I've loved for years when faced with blatant stupidity: Lord, put your arm around my shoulders and your hand over my mouth. That has saved me many times from striking down someone who isn't evil, just stumbling through life with the wrong DNA.

I hope when I'm pushing 80, (remember I was maybe 42 when I wrote this, and I'm 86 now!) if I'm lucky enough to live that long, that there's a 50-year-old somewhere nearby who loves me and makes sure I have a cab or takes my arm when the sidewalk is uneven. I know my energy and love of a productive life is stimulating and fun for my older friends, who by choice lead gentler, more sedentary lives.

Let's go back to Mom. My beautiful mother, and she is a very beautiful woman, has always been younger than Springtime. I admit, I was shocked when one day I realized that Mother had become elderly, at least in terms of age. She too was shocked, and we both had to get used to the idea that she physically wasn't 40 anymore, didn't bounce back as quickly, and had to modify her lifestyle to allow time to regenerate. Okay, we went through that, even got through the frightening hurdle of a mastectomy in her 73rd year.

But ten years before that, she complained about her own looks. "Look at what I've done to myself—sun wrinkles on top of sun wrinkles (remember, we lived in South Florida). I feel 50 but look like I'm 80 or more." So, my wife and I, then living in Buenos Aires, Argentina, gave Mom a most unusual Christmas Present

—a Facelift with Argentina's premier plastic surgeon. The net net? She looked 15 to 20 years younger than her actual age of 65.

A funny remembrance: Just three weeks after surgery we all went to a massive cocktail party, and mother artfully arranged some netting so the surgery, now healing, wouldn't show. During the party, she came over to us, my likeable Stepdad standing with me, and said, "Oh darling, don't come over, it's such fun—there's a 40-year-old trying to pick me up. Don't worry, he won't succeed, but he's sure making your 65-year-old wife smile a lot."

Now what? Mom lives every day cheerfully. She has her moments of being bugged by age, but certainly doesn't have the mindset of someone living her last day, week, month, or year on earth. She still paints. She still travels, comes up to New York to see me and catch a few of the provocative plays on Broadway. I remember when she was about 80, we went to a very hot socio/comedy drama on Broadway. The leading lady was on a sofa in the living room and the leading man entered from stage right, put his hand on her knee and under her skirt, touching her in all the inappropriate places. I thought, this is probably not the most suitable play to see with your aging mother, but she smiled, and said, "Thank goodness I have only short-term memory loss."

She'll spend the holidays at Troutbeck, my country inn, and woo and win more new friends every year. She is exactly what she should be--a completely contemporary woman who happens to be in her late 70's. (And was still a Big-Time Favorite of all my friends when she was in her 80's). And remember that face-lift we gifted her—she looked maybe 70 when she finally went to her maker at, my goodness, at my present age: 85.

So much for Mother's young point of view. The reason I want to dwell on Mothers and Parents is that it's a terribly important part of the aging process. You always hurt the ones you love. That's true of parents and children too. If you've been blessed with a decent and loving parent who did the very best he or she could do during your formative years, then it's time for the big payback.

If ever there's a time when you shouldn't have major financial worries, or emotional harassment of any sort, it's when you're elderly. So, if you're a kid, and are impatient with your parents, and don't want to take the time to make their life better, then do them a favor, make sure they're all right financially, and then leave them alone.

Who knows, maybe you think your parents weren't terrific. Maybe you truthfully don't love them. As hard as it might be, perhaps the best thing you could do for them would be to admit your real feelings and tell them you'll leave them in peace. I know that's a tough point of view. Guess I've seen too many people living under a Fake Blue Sky.

Giving false lip service to your role as a loving son or daughter can be the most damaging thing in the world to an older parent who doesn't understand why you're treating them so badly.

I had one friend who admitted that his mother had always been a pain in the you know what. Never happy, never productive, never supportive— "She was just whining, miserable, demanding, and destructive. But," he said, "she is my mother, so, I've set her up financially. She doesn't have to worry about paying the bills. I drag her to the family Seder every year, and that's it. I even send her a present on her birthday. She knows I'm not crazy about her, but also knows I recognize her as my mother. And not caring a lot about her, didn't stop me from finding an excellent retirement home for her, where she has lots of little old lady friends she can complain to and tell them what a terrible son she has."

Frankly, comparing his edgy Mother/Son relationship compared to my Love-and-Respect Mother/Son relationship, I always felt sorry for them. Recently, his unloved mother went to her glory, and at the funeral, no one offered to say a few words about her. So, my friend took the podium and startled family members by saying,

"I wish I could tell you some wonderful, loving, happy memories of Mother--but there are none. The best we can hope and pray for is that she has now found the peace and happiness in death that she never knew in life."

I know I'm digressing from a story about Mom, but not really. This brings me to perhaps one of the most important points I want to make about aging. If you live your life right up to the last moment with a loving, sharing, giving viewpoint, you will always be missed, always remembered, talked about, thought about. Someone will always think of you and shed a tear or smile. What a wonderful legacy. Just think of that poor woman who died. No one cared. I'm sure no one ever mentions her anymore. She was just a stain on a rug and was removed.

The parent child relationship works both ways. A kid can be a rotter and so can a parent. EVERYONE at one time or another complains about his or her parents. And sometimes, like the sad old lady mentioned above, the complaints are justified. Take a close look at yourself-- are you a pain in the neck? Are you spending all your days complaining and whining, demanding and accusing, creating guilt and torment instead of tenderness?

Ask yourself these questions: Would you want to be your friend? Do you smile a lot? Are you concerned, really concerned about your friends? Are you alert about what's going on in the world? Do you still make interesting conversation? Does your house look the way it should look? Are you as well-groomed as you can be? Do you remember to do the small loving things for friends?

Do you Listen? Yeah, I mean really listen—not just Hear your children or your friends when they're talking to you--do you honestly listen to what they're saying, what they're trying to tell you? We were born to listen, to our mothers and fathers, our doctors, our bosses, our friends. And face it—you wouldn't have anything to say unless there was someone there to Listen to you. I want you to think about that the next time someone important in your life calls. Block out all other thoughts and listen to them. Amazing what you might learn. I liked a quote from Calvin Coolidge: "A man never listened himself out of a job."

How long has it been since you wrote a short, loving note to a friend--or even more important, to one of your children? Do you love your children? Why? Why not? And have you told them lately? Have you *ever* told them you love them? Don't look amazed, many people in the world never ever say those three magic words, I love you.

It took me many years to understand that my take-charge attitude, my ability to cope with problems, my love of life, was all a reflection of a loving and intelligent mother. Not that my father wasn't terrific, and I'm sure was a powerful influence on who and what I am, but remember, I was only a young 14 when he left this world. Fortunately, Mom and I share an outlook on life which works well for us. We are helpful, loving people. We expect the best out of people and of course usually get it. We feel blessed when someone loves us, so we try to live up to their love—you know, make it all worthwhile for them.

(All this part, and leading up to it, was part of the original manuscript.) Obviously, I don't need a Mommy. I'm very much in charge of my own life. And I know (and so does she) that she won't live forever. But for the remaining years, and I hope there are lots and lots of them, we're going to remain friends, good loving friends, who delight in each other's triumphs, and will try to soften one another's sorrows. When Mom heads for St. Peter's Gates, my life won't end. I'll have the happy memory of her. I'll also know that I made the last "bumpety" years of her life more comfortable, more satisfying, more exciting, more worthwhile. It's the big payback, and I'm so glad I can be on the giving end. One thing I am doing with her now (and continued doing until her death many years later) is to call her at 5 pm every day, just to hear her voice, share a theatre review, discuss politics, the weather, whatever, and it anchors both of us.

Wherever you are at this very moment, Mother, I hope you are having a happy, productive, affection-filled day. Here's a big hug and kiss from your kid.

I'm smiling, reading this chapter, knowing I wrote it around 1977, like 44 years ago. And my Five-Star Relationship with Mom went on happily for many years —until 1994—I was 59, and Mom was 85, when we said our last goodbyes, still smiling at one another.

One of the best reasons I have for remembering Mom was her insistence on my understanding and living by The Golden Rule. So, as I told you before, I rewrote it— for myself and my daughters. Just five words, and three of them are four-letter words. No, not those four-letter words, there are some good ones: Love, Help, Pray, Save. Anyway, I'm repeating my Golden Rule again because it's important and could make your life much easier: ***YOU GET WHAT YOU GIVE.*** Think about that. If you give a helping hand, a sympathetic ear, a generous heart, a loving hug—guess what—you get that back. But if all you do is Criticize and complain and gossip and cheat—you get that back too. Think about it again. Give Good—and you Get Good. Sure makes life easier.

Daughters and Me. Most of you have children and I hope you're glad. If you can think back far enough, remember the total care necessary for the infant months, the growing, needing baby, the loud, often whining small child, the never totally neat house. Why did we all do that to ourselves? I'm kidding. I hope you had children because you wanted to have children.

I also remember the delight of seeing them conquer the scariness of starting school, and often winning that daily challenge—not just learning, but also learning how to relate to their own age group. I remember too, the delight of rocking them to sleep, singing songs. Then, older, of discussing books with them, or traveling. Our first foreign excursion was Ireland, England, and France. We cruised home on the S.S. United States. And years later, climbed through Machu Picchu with them as we explored all South America while we were living in Argentina.

And more than anything, now, just having turned 86, I can't imagine NOT having children. My babies are about 60 now, but still seem to love me most of the time and feel confident enough to lecture me (and I try not to laugh at them). I don't want to live with either of them and am reasonably sure they don't want to live with me —but you know something—if we had to wake up every day under the same roof, it would be okay.

Remember—your children exist because you wanted them to exist. I'm glad their college education didn't match the cost of today's universities. I've helped pay off some college debts for the Grandsons. But I'm happy to see all four grandsons love their mothers. The boys have a friendly albeit distant relationship with me, which is fine. They please me, and I'm fascinated to see what's going to happen with my Great Grandson, an incredibly handsome Anglo-Asian lad (his Mommy is a lovely Japanese girl) only 4 now. He'll end up in some government's Cabinet or marry royalty. I mean, look at his DNA! As of today, another Great Grandchild is on the way!

Okay, that's a lot about families. If that's all the goodness you can take at one time, let's switch gears and talk about Passion. Yeah, Passion!

Chapter Six

THE IMPORTANCE OF PASSION

*"If I had known I was going to live this long,
I would have taken better care of myself."*

NOW NOW, DON'T BE confused by the title. This isn't one of those kisses and tell books. I'm talking about a much more lasting passion—an interest in something that really counts in your life. Years ago, I read a quote from a great British artist/writer/performer, Noel Coward, and I totally agreed with him and have lived my life with his terrific observation: **"Work is much more fun than fun."**

For example, business is a big passion at a certain time in your life—solving the problems, making the money, scoring big in the boardroom. Nowadays, that's a passion shared by both men and women of all races and skin colors. It pleases me to see that.

Back when we were all kids, the passion of business was a male fraternity. Nowadays, for the ladies, those who are not career bent, their children become an overriding passion. Or sometimes, a husband becomes a woman's major passion in life. And then there's the one woman I know who said, "Bridge is the only worthwhile passion." For her, she's probably right.

So here you are with time on your hands. Well, it's true—idle hands are the Devil's playground, and just to make things worse, you don't have the energy to let the Devil have his (or her) way. Time to get busy and discover a new passion.

Back years ago, a little old lady in New England named Grandma Moses astounded the art world by becoming one of its brightest stars even though she was well "over the hill". Wonder why everyone was amazed?! Why can't you still be brilliant at anything you do, no matter what your age? Good Lord, you have an inner peace that comes from knowing yourself all these years. Try to discover the Hidden You. You might be in for a big surprise. At any rate, how does one make that discovery? I think you can do it via a process of elimination.

Make a list of all the things that one can do with one's free time. These are in no order of importance: Let's create the list together:

1. Paint.

2. Make Jewelry (Arts & Crafts)

3. Write (it's hard, believe me)

4. Counsel other, troubled elders

5. Church work

6. Start a business

7. Get a college degree or graduate degree

8. Travel, & when you do, make notes about your travels, and write articles for AARP and other books devoted to Seniors.

9. If it's in you, do volunteer work. Handicapped children need a lot. Volunteer at your local hospital.

10. Learn how to swim. Take Golf lessons. Take up Tennis.

11. Learn bridge

12. Study a foreign language—but really become fluent in it.

13. If you don't live in a metropolitan center where you can find courses for any and everything, take a correspondence course in something that you have always wanted to do. Maybe become an interior designer. Even if no one hires you for a big job, wouldn't it be exciting if you could improve your knowledge of color and texture, and how to make them live happily together?

14. Fall in love with fine art. Make the great museums of this and every country as familiar as your kitchen table. Don't just look—learn to understand art.

15. Become a music lover.

16. Make theatre and the cinema your bailiwick. That's tough if you don't live in a metropolitan center, but it's not impossible.

17. Join a book club.

18. Get a pet.

We can certainly add to the list, but for the moment, these are enough passions to start with. Now let's take a brief look at each one of them and figure out which is "you".

1.Painting. Never could draw a circle you say, or a straight line? Couldn't color within the lines? Good. Maybe in your heart of hearts you have an impressionist's softly distorted view of life. To paint, there's a small investment necessary. You must buy paints, some paper palettes, some stretched canvasses, a couple of brushes, palette knives, probably an easel. But I'm getting ahead of myself. Check with all the high schools in the area and find out which one is offering adult education courses at nighttime. Or ask at a senior citizen's center if anyone is teaching painting. I know I had my first series of painting lessons (I was 32) at a high school in the evenings, and really loved it, and turned out some decent, if not award-winning oils for my efforts.

My lovely and loving mother, today, at 76, is still painting and teaching painting. She lives in an "adult community" in Melbourne, Florida, with her best friends living next door. They all got smart and set up their own support system for their late years. And Mom is the painting teacher for the community. What does she charge? $4 a lesson—and that's for three hours. She says, "we're all living with some limited finances, and truthfully I'd do it for nothing, but then they wouldn't listen to me." After about six lessons, her pupils, many of whom have never held a brush, have a finished painting to hang in their own home. You can't imagine the satisfaction of producing your own painting. It's such an exciting passion, and it's something you can do all by yourself. Yes, it's fun to get together with someone and paint, but you can sit in your own home, (standing is better, and better for you) and create. It's a thrilling thing to do with your time.

Perhaps you'll like watercolors, but I suggest oils because they're easier—if you make a mistake you can paint over it or rub it out. You don't know what talent lies inside you until you give it a chance to fly. I've seen elders from all financial walks of life take up painting and all have agreed it's changed their lives. One of those friends sells her oils (she studied with someone very important) for about $1,500 a canvas. My mother doesn't fetch those kinds of bucks for her paintings, but she gave me a large, beautiful painting of irises last Christmas...and it's terrific, really is. It's hanging in our important guest bedroom. Ex-President George Bush is getting kudos (praise!) for his portraits; and Winston Churchill's paintings are collector's items.

2. Make jewelry. Why did I include this? Well, I think arts and crafts are some of the best things you can do. First, they force the right-hand side of your brain—the creative side—to really get cracking; in most cases they don't require an enormous investment of money; and the finished results are very satisfying.

Making jewelry is just one of these types of things. Making models, like ship models, or building a miniature model of the house you grew up in, or perhaps making shell mirrors as a friend of mine does. Either buy a cheap mirror with a broad flat frame and glue imaginative things to it (I saw one made of dried noodles and spaghetti and it was great looking), or if someone in the family or coterie of friends is handy, have them build you a simple box frame, and then you can create the frame out of any material you choose. Making jewelry usually requires a lesson from someone. Your local high schools are a good source for arts/crafts/painting/adult education classes. The damn virus may restrict some of these. Stringing beads and shells are fun. I have a friend who does it professionally. So, I bought a whole selection of beads, shells, and the tools, and she taught my mother, who now makes beautiful necklaces, many of which she has sold.

---

3. Write. Aaargh. Not sure if I want all the competition that's lurking out there. But it's a big ocean, so come on in. You can try writing on your own with no lessons. Who knows—you may become the Erma Bombeck of the geriatric set? There are a zillion little publications that just might love to publish what you write, and some might even pay for it. With or without pay, it's wonderful to see something in print with your byline on it.

What to write about? Life! What you've done, what you do, why you do it, how to cook it, how to lose weight, how to gain weight, how to raise tulips (or as a friend of mine said, how to destroy tulips), how to get along with obstreperous grandchildren, how you overcame depression, why opera has changed your life, the importance of having and loving a pet and of course this list could be 150 pages long.

Even though writing is something you can try all on your own, if you feel the need to have lessons, you'll find courses in creative writing taught in the adult education centers (local high schools), or in a local junior college or university. Or if you live in Smalltown, America (as I do), and nothing is nearby, there are many wonderful correspondence and on-line courses, for writing novel, short stories, blogs (like essays), even poetry.

Ask Google about what's out there and prepare to be amazed at the multitude of choices. And if you really have a book, fiction or non-fiction inside of you, go online right now and look for Self-Publishing School. They're terrific people and are one of the reasons you're reading this book! Another terrific way to juice up your writing—find a Writer's Group. I still belong to one, and we love to discuss a new assignment every week with one another. And those cost nothing but a few creative hours a week. In our group of eight, most are over 70, at least three of us in our 80s. Some of them are more talented than they realize. They may never earn a dime from their "essays" but what a treasure to leave for your children and grandchildren.

Although I've lived my life as a writer (and loved every word), I had a sign over my desk in NYC for years: *Writing is Easy. You just stare at a blank piece of paper (or screen these days) until drops of blood appear on your forehead.*

---

4. Counsel others. What do I mean by that? Just what it says. You may think you have it tough, but believe me friend, there are a million people out there who have it a lot rougher and tougher than you. Do you still have reasonably good eyesight? What if you were going blind? Why don't you call the Lighthouse for the Blind and ask if you can volunteer as a reader? If you've had a mastectomy, and your doctor says you are bone clean of the cancer, find out about the organization of women who go into the hospitals and talk to new mastectomy patients, mentally devastated and shattered by the surgery. You'll be thrilled to find how much hope you can give them.

If you had (or think you have) a drinking problem, find one of the many AA meetings in your community and go meet some of the smartest, interesting people in the world. And besides solving your own problems, you'll learn how to help others.

Hey guy, you were such a big gun in the business world—what makes you think all those years don't count for something? There's an organization in most major metropolitan areas comprising retirees who advise baby businesses. Become a mentor. You'll be happy to have something worthwhile to do, and as you know, there's nothing sexier than business. Are you getting the idea? Think about your background, your training, and how much expertise you could share with other people. You'll probably make some new friends and have a lot of fun for yourself at the same time.

---

5. Church work. Getting a little closer to God certainly can't hurt. And goodness knows the Church can use your goodness. There's always a lot to do, people to help, funds to raise, recreation halls and altars to decorate, a rector, priest or rabbi who might need your helping hand. A Church is like a diamond. It has many facets, and they all need to be polished regularly. (This is current news, in the year 2020): A good Catholic Boy I'm not anymore, but I am a good and regular church-member. I found a Minister I love, (all of us in the congregation love him) and I sing in the choir. It's a Presbyterian Church. But a Catholic priest friend of mine agreed with me when I asked, Does God really care where we sing and pray as long as we continue to sing and pray? Spending a couple of hours each week talking to your Lord can be very healthy and uplifting. By the way, my Presbyterian Church recently anointed me as an Elder, to help guide the church and its investments and property. It's a serious obligation.

---

6. Start a business. What! Now that I'm retired, I should make myself crazy with another business? Why not? It can be a small business. It doesn't have to make a ton of money. Maybe you can take one of the funsy things you like to do, like learning how to make jewelry and turn that into a business. How? Make a commune out of your best buddies. Figure out how many necklaces or picture frames or whatever it is you can make, and then go out and find a buyer for them. Somewhere, there's a store that will take everything you can produce. Or if you knit beautifully, make glorious knitted things and find a boutique in town that will take all your production. You could even organize a group of knitters. A friend of mine did it and was very successful. Start a babysitting business. You can find other gals like yourself who are willing. You can make the contacts and the bookings, and of course, you'll make something on every job.

---

7. Get a college degree or graduate degree. I have not flipped out. You're never too old to improve your mind. And God knows, there's nothing like a final exam to make the heart beat faster. All the studying would be wonderful for you. Pushing yourself mentally is great for staying young. And think how fascinating to be with fine professors and to share the excitement of learning with all your younger co-students (who would undoubtedly come to love you).

It would open a million new doors for you, you'd meet some exciting, worthwhile people, and remove yourself from any elderly status. You'd be just another student, even though a student with a few more years of life experiences. At this age and stage, your degree doesn't have to lead you into a lifetime career. It would be enough just to become an educated expert on something that really matters to you. You like archeology? Terrific

—get your degree in it! Art history is your thing? Political science? Foreign cultures? American literature? There is no wrong choice. And of course, you can do it all on-line if there isn't a nearby community college.

---

8. Travel. I'm thinking of a couple I knew and admired. I thought, really believed they were in their mid-fifties They both were trim, quick to laugh, ready for adventure on a moment's notice. Even the hair color was natural, and they had less grey than I did in my 36-year-old head. We had all gone snorkeling that day, off the coast of Columbia, and although it wasn't truly perilous, we were snorkeling next to an active reef, with reasonably strong wave action, and lots of dangerous fire coral just below our floating bodies.

Later that same day, the lady and I had found a trail leading up a hill across an adventurous island, and took a long, productive walk, trying to identify the local flora and fauna collecting choice pieces of coral on the way. She told me she had made shell mirrors for their home in the islands, a modest cottage they had bought years ago. They were residents of a large commuting city near New York. She had had painting exhibits, and now was into metal sculptures. No, she wasn't a big-time trained artist —she just did anything that seemed interesting and worthwhile.

That night during cocktails (we had discovered a lethal one called a Pelican Smash—I was a controlled drinker in all those young days—didn't drink during the working day, and nowadays, drink nothing except flavored seltzers) their son came up in conversation. The other couple traveling with us, 48 and 40 respectively, mentioned something about our new friends' son, who was apparently a respected surgeon, and only 38 years old. I remember thinking, wow--if he was 38, unless they married as teenagers, they were at least 60. Turns out they had married late and were both just barely shy of 70.

Ah wonderment. We, in our mid 30s spent five days with those two comfortable loving zanies, playing bridge with them every evening, and exploring unchartered islands during the day. I can't remember traveling with two people who were easier to be with or as relaxed or as willing to do something interesting. Okay you say that's easy for them. Apparently blessed with great energy and a young outlook, what about those of us who show and feel our age, even though we are mentally willing and desirous of traveling? Well, there are some no-no's about traveling.

Let's review: Traveling can be exhausting and even dangerous. If you have high blood pressure, or an existing heart condition, don't put yourself in an uncomfortable and possibly dangerous environment. For example, when I lived in South America, and traveled around a lot with my family, I often noticed large tour groups, consisting mainly of elderly people, traveling where they shouldn't have been. Machu Picchu, Peru, for instance, is one of the great wonders of the world but getting there requires a vigorous body and spirit. First, you go to Cuzco, which is about 12,000 feet in altitude. Even a healthy person suffers from altitude headaches. Your breath comes short, you're exhausted. The trip to Machu Picchu is an adventure by rail that could be a scene in "Around the World in 80 Days!" Once there, it requires tremendous stamina to climb up and down that magic village of rocks built so long ago. It could be deadly. So, before you book anything, make sure it won't make physical demands that your body will refuse to meet.

If you are fair fair fair and have overly delicate skin, forget about the beauty of the islands. The sun would kill you—it's omni-present, everywhere. Instead, go visit some other islands—the lovely and relaxing countryside of the United Kingdom and stay in England's posh inns, or enjoy the myriad of small, beautiful pleasures in country Ireland, Wales or Scotland. My only hesitation would be if dampness reminds you of your arthritis or rheumatism. If not, you'll love the British Isles. While you're on that side of the pond (a funny expression I think), why not go motoring through the vineyard countryside of France where you'll enjoy some of the finest foods and wines in the world. If you don't mind cool or cold weather, take an off-season vacation—there are fewer crowds, and you don't feel rushed or pushed. I recall seeing Holland one Christmas. My memories of Amsterdam are with Christmas decorations, and the beautiful canals partially frozen over.

And there are many quiet vacation spots where the emphasis is on no stress, no ties, no schedule. just a delicate quality of life.

My own country inn and conference center, Troutbeck, just two hours north of Manhattan, nicely qualified, and there are thousands of others. *(A note about Troutbeck. I developed it with just one partner, and I ran it for 30 years. Am happy to say we sold it in 2016, and the new owners brought a new level of sophistication to the operation. It's still very much a lovely destination if you want to treat yourselves to a sophisticated weekend or wedding or conference with a lot of comfort and fine cuisine.... look it up at Troutbeck.com).*

If you still seek a foreign adventure, investigate the AARP tours, age-conscious with acceptable schedules, which can be important when you're older, offering enough time between stopovers to get your bearings, without feeling you're on the run all the time. And let's not forget Cruises. Cruises are an excellent choice when the years have been adding up. It's mighty nice to be in a floating country club with all the amenities and usually some interesting people as well. Be careful not to overeat and drink. There's an abundance of both.

If you want some personal guidance about a trip, send me a note to P O Box 26, Amenia, New York, 12501 I'd love to hear from you. I've traveled a lot and have happy memories about much of the world. Always smart is to enlist a professional travel agent for tickets, reservations, and excursions. You don't know a travel agent? My favorite is an expert named Vivian de Leon. Her email address is: viviand@vwti.com. And forgetting travel for the moment, it doesn't really matter where you live. *There is no Wrong choice---it's how you live, not where you live.*

---

9. Volunteer. Yeah, Give. Give yourself to your hospital, to your schools, to a homeless center. Somewhere, someone needs You. And if you look around your community and make a few calls, you won't believe how many opportunities there are for you to bring an appreciative smile to someone's face.

---

10. Learn how to swim. Learn how to swim. Say it with me: Learn How to Swim. Shame on you. I can't believe you don't know. Everyone should know how to swim and certainly no one teaches it better than the good old Red Cross or YMCA. Then, once you know how to swim, join the local Y or a health club, and use that new ability. Swimming, and water exercises are among the best low-stress things you can do for your not-so-young body. And of course, it's fun too. Now, in my 86th year, I depend on my 30 minutes a day in the pool every morning, staying limber. Besides not wanting to walk like an old man, it's good for the rest of me.

Take up tennis. Too active you say. Balderdash I say. You don't have to play at Wimbledon. Tennis makes you use your muscles and move around a court. You swing, you force more air into your lungs, you move your body around the court. An hour of tennis might be more than enough and will certainly give you all the exercise you need, and it's a delightful game.

Let's include golf in this discussion. Man or woman, golf is wonderful. It gets you out in the fresh air, you stroll about handsome green fields, and you learn how to properly address your ball, and how to give it a good whack. Also, it's fun to meet people on the 19th green (there are only 18 for you non-golfers) and swap golf tales.

If you live in the tropics, do something that might make your children wonder about your sanity (or envy you). *Learn how to scuba dive.* Did you see the movie,

Cocoon? You'll see some senior citizens scuba-ing. Of course, it's easier to just go snorkeling, but why not learn scuba? It costs a little more, so don't attempt it if you're on a very limited income. *Other things to take up: dancing, pool/billiards, piano, you complete this list.*

11.Learn bridge. I didn't bunch bridge in with all those other things you can learn to do because I think it's worth a mention all by itself. Bridge is a wonderful game. Every hand is completely different. And like all card games, it has an element of luck, some days you get all the good hands, and other days…well, you know. But more than luck, bridge is skill. It makes you think, and therefore I think is a better game. It doesn't let you get mentally lazy.

Bridge makes you think about what you're doing and remember what cards have been played. It also allows you to have a group of friends. It's a nice social time. Scout around your town. Perhaps one of the women's clubs will offer bridge lessons, or adult education or the Y, or if there's absolutely nothing, get some bridge playing friends to teach you. They'll be glad to make you a convert. And don't tell me you prefer Solitaire.

---

12. Study a foreign language. Now I don't mean take a quickie course. I mean really learn it—become fluent in another language. You can't imagine how satisfying it is to handle another language with ease. Living in South America forced me to make room in my head for Spanish. I fought the process but am delighted I lost the war. I still love speaking Spanish, and it's a rare week that I don't use it, if but for a few minutes. My daughters still speak it too. Think how delightful it is to travel to a foreign country and speak with the natives. It's good for you and your self-image. Wonder if I'm too old to learn Italian or French?

---

13. Correspondence courses. Very very pleasing, and I know I've mentioned them before, but they're worth your focus! There are correspondence courses on absolutely everything in the world these days. So, if you don't have museums handy or junior colleges or high schools or YMCA or Red Cross or senior citizen centers, ask Google about correspondence courses on your computer or iPad or even your cell phone. It's that easy. Just write in the Google search bar: Who offers correspondence courses on _____ (pick the subject OR subjects that interest you!)

And here are a few to check. This is just a tiny list. And they may have all that you need. But once you start looking on-line, you'll discover the list and opportunities are endless.

- *Study.com*

- *Distance—education.org*

- *WiseGeek.com*

---

14. Fine Art. Best of all, if there are museums handy, go to them. Even if you're in a wheelchair or using a walker, walking through a museum looking at someone's soul exposed on canvas, will make you think. Then, visit local galleries. Good Lord, you know that name—you did not know she was so talented! Or, if that painting is good enough to be in a gallery, why can't you paint? Recently I sold one of our homes to a famous contemporary artist. I am not a contemporary art collector. But knowing him forced me into studying contemporary art more closely, and I feel my artistic boundaries expanding. Now, read #1 above, about Painting, and start finding your artistic soul.

---

15. Become a Music Lover. Oh sure, you loved the music of your period, whether it was the melodic 50s or the wham-bam of rock n' roll, or hip-hop, or even rap (I still don't understand it). Music seduces the mind. Have you ever gone to a symphony orchestra concert? Oh, Dear God, the richness, the brilliance, the magic produced by Violins and Cellos and French horns and Bassoons and Oboes and Clarinets and Flutes and Trumpets and Drums (okay, Percussion) will enrich your blood flow, and clarify your mindset. If you have a smart-alecky mouth as I, you might call it, hmmm, refined sex.

I'd be interested in your description of what it does to your mind and body. How to be a music lover? Tune-in. Go to any available concerts. Or listen on-line. Take a music course, in person if available. Even though I've earned my living as a writer (and innkeeper), I played clarinet, cello, and Bassoon in high school. And that Bassoon then paid for my college tuition. No, I don't play any instrument anymore, but I have an ongoing affection for all kinds of music.

———

16.Theater. I like to spell it Theatre. Have you ever been in a local production? Talk about boosting your heartbeat. And the first time you hear Applause, you'll understand why so many people spend their entire lives trying to get up on the stage. Okay, maybe you're not a performer, but reading about theatre is entertaining and educational and fun. It's another subject you can study at home, although there's nothing like sitting in a dark theatre and listening to the overture of a musical, or watch the curtain rise to a dark drama of despair.

If you can get a group of friends together, get the manuscript of a play and everyone takes a part and you read it. Wow. It sure beats getting together for coffee and a donut. And I'm not going to poo-poo television. There have been TV series that will thrill you. If you didn't see Aaron Sorkin's THE WEST WING about the White House, you missed one of the best things every written (and performed) for TV. I think you can find it for free on Netflix. And if surgical scenes don't upset you, the soap-opera antics of GREY'S ANATOMY will make you wish you had gone to medical school and give you a few leads on how to talk to your own doctors. THE QUEEN'S GAMBIT will surprise you—so excellent. And gents, especially you, don't miss THE KOMINSKY METHOD. Great laughs, and at our age, very understandable.

---

17. Join a Book Club. I know you like to read, but you can't imagine the fun when all 3 or 10 of you are reading the Same Book, and then get together and really discuss it. Suddenly you know why Lucille dropped whatshisname and took up with Harry. You'll learn while reading. If you can't find a group handy, start one yourself. Just call four or five friends, tell them your plan, and get together and choose between two or three books to get started. Such fun.

---

18. Get a Pet. No, I'm not kidding. Unless you have a built-in dislike of dogs or cats, you can't imagine how much joy they bring to your life. Not just company, a pet is Loving Company, non-judgmental and always ready to cuddle or curl up next to you for a siesta. Yes, they are a responsibility. And if trained right, they may take themselves out for bathroom duty. Of if your health agrees, it's good for you to take a walk twice a day with your best friend, Stardust or BigBoy—well, you can pick better names than those. Okay, is that enough passion? Now let's go back to my passion—Words. I love words, love to read them, love to write them. And I've found some wonderful articles that are so full of wisdom, I want to share them with you right now.

Okay, is that enough passion?

Chapter Seven

WONDERFUL WORDS AND THOUGHTS FROM PEOPLE WORTH LISTENING TO

"When an elder dies, a library burns to the ground." (African proverb)

I SUBSCRIBE (IT'S FREE!) to a wonderful daily log that I highly recommend to you. A gentleman I know only through his writing, Mr. Chip Conley, has live-in seminars in a blissful setting in the Baja of Mexico. He calls it the Modern Elder Academy, which is geared to helping people, some your age, some a trifle younger, re-energize their lives, helps them find a new direction. But he also sends out a daily blog full of his own excellent observations and others he's researched.

Here's one I want to include in my love letter to you'uns.

The Psychological Formula for Success After Age 50. (From Bloomberg BusinessWeek)

Don't be scared by the title. Chip says the heart of this article is this: "Grit" is the secret ingredient for an exceptional third act.

Psychologists have long known that success is fueled by grit, passion, and a growth mindset—a deep-seated conviction that you can excel at a new pursuit. Norwegian psychologist Hermundur Sigmundsson says that passion is by far the most important psychological factor—but it peaks early. To a lesser extent, the same is true of the growth mindset, so by the time most of us reach the "Build a Company Phase" of our life, two of the three most important ingredients in the recipe for achievement are waning. "You lost the thinking that maybe you can do this," Sigmundsson says.

Fortunately, grit—that combination of perseverance and determination—rises through middle age and peaks in your 70s as do a number of other helpful intellectual traits, including your ability to perceive the emotional state of other people. Even your vocabulary, comprehension, and aptitude for math keep climbing until at least 50. Here are four suggestions from the Bloomberg article on how to be more effective at work after the age of 50:

1. **Make it Meaningful.** *Once you pass the half-century mark, avoid work you don't find compelling. The pandemic provides the perfect occasion to ditch —or be fired from—a position that doesn't do much beyond keeping the lights on and the fridge full. As one person says, "Take all the good from your past ventures and throw them into the future."*

2. **Move Your Body.** *"Physical activity is very important to keep the gray and white matter in your grain more functional," says Sigmundsson. His studies show that successful older people are all physically active, including everyone mentioned in this article. Anything that gets your heart pumping, such as walking, swimming, yoga, boxing or weights, will do the trick.*

3. **Fight weakness.** *Which is lowest: your grit, passion or growth mindset? Help nurture your weakest trait by surrounding yourself with people and deadlines that bolster it. If your entrepreneurial passion is fading, find an enthusiastic business partner and join an incubator program. If you fear you won't be able to write that novel you keep seeing*

*in your dreams, join a weekly writing group and hire a book coach. **(A personal note, friends. Go on-line and look at Self-PublishingSchool.com. A great source if your brain is hiding a book.)***

4. ***Beyond Work****. Bonus points for learning completely new skills, which can improve cognitive function. The more novel and mentally demanding, the better—say learning a new language or musical instrument.*

Another wonderful article from Mr. Conley: Are We All Washed-Up After 50?

This question affects a growing number of mid-lifers who feel like a brown banana in the produce stand—well past its sell-by date. But a publication in the New England Journal of medicine (2018) found that the most productive age in a human's life is not in our 20s or 30s, but between the ages of 60 and 70.

The study confirmed that the second most productive age is between 70 and 80 and the third most productive decade is 50 to 60. *What the heck? Why isn't this front-page news? And, yet, as outlined in this Forbes article,* *the number of US. People 55 and older who are participating in the workforce is down by 2 million.*

Here are a few other facts worth noting:

- *The average age of a Nobel Prize winner is 62.*
- *The average age of a CEO in a Fortune 50 company is 63.*
- *The average age of the pastors of the 100 biggest churches in America is 71.*
- *The average age for a Pope is 76.*

Corporate management has traditionally viewed productivity as 'how many widgets does one person make in an hour?' Of course, this industrial model of productivity is ready for retirement as a variety of variables now need to be considered in the modern workplace. Everything from how a worker helps improve everyone around them to the quality of the widgets produced. There's also growing evidence that older workers offer an 'invisible productivity' that makes them more effective, namely their life wisdom, emotional intelligence, and ability to create psychological safety. These things matter.

Go on your computer or cell phone and look at wisdomwell@modernelderacademy.com and put yourself on their mailing list. You won't regret it. And if you have the time, investigate one of Mr. Conley's Modern Elder Academy weeks dedicated to reviving your interest in yourself and the world around you. Sounds like fun, more affordable than not, and would be chock full of good thinking for a slightly aging body and mind.

I don't know who said this final quote, but I think it's worth remembering.

> *"Today is the oldest you've ever been, yet it's also the youngest you'll ever be — so enjoy every minute of it."*

Chapter Eight

THIS IS NOT GOODBYE

"Everybody is who he was in High School."

M Y DEAR OLD FRIENDS•••MY God, how much I love and need you all. Each one of you. You've given me hope when my world looked bleak. You've shared your wisdom when I was in sore need. You've shared your love and offered it to me, asking, wanting, or expecting nothing in return. I hope I gave something back. But I want you to know how much you have always meant to me, and what you will continue to mean to me.

And when the time comes for you to go to your glory, please know that no one will shed a more heartfelt tear, and perhaps no one will mourn less. Less? How's that? Okay, we all know that we do not and will not live forever. But we can prolong the joy of living by living more wisely, taking better care of ourselves, and best of all, living every moment of every day in a productive and meaningful way. And if you do all that, if someone really loves you, besides missing you terribly for years and years to come, they shouldn't mourn long, because they'll be concentrating on all the wonderful things you have always been. That's what I do. I concentrate on the fun we had, the thousand laughs, the memories, the hugs, the caring. And I guess I want everyone to do that.

Excessive mourning is a bore and doesn't pay tribute to the deceased. I honestly believe that if you live *This Isn't Goodbye* right, you go right on living forever, cheerfully, in someone's mind and heart. And isn't that worthwhile?! If you know me, you know how much I care for you. And if you don't, I hope these words have helped you find out something about yourself and perhaps given you a new point of view for the days and weeks and months and years and probably decades ahead.

Back to my love of words. One of my favorite Authors is an Authoress named Elizabeth Gilbert. You probably know her best for her (I believe) fifth book,

EAT PRAY LOVE, which she wrote to help her analyze herself. OH, she's so brilliant. That's such a wonderful book (and a delightful film—do see it). One of her newest books is a surprising let's-have-a-party jaunt through NYC in the 40s and 50s, titled CITY OF GIRLS. It's another extraordinary example of her unending talent. And it's all told from the viewpoint of a very elderly lady. At one point, she says (and I want you to read and think about it): *"This is what I've found about life, as I've gotten older: you start to lose people. It's not that there is ever a shortage of people—oh, heavens no. It is merely that—as the years pass—there comes to be a terrible shortage of your people. The ones you loved. The ones who knew the people that you both loved. The ones who know your whole history.*

Those people start to be plucked away by death, and they are awfully hard to replace after they go. After a certain age, it can become difficult to make new friends. The world can begin to feel lonely and sparse, teeming though it may be with freshly minted young souls.

I'm not sure whether you've had that feeling yet. But I've had it. And you may have that feeling someday." Worth thinking about, right?

You get only one shot at life, friends, so let's none of us waste it. I'd like to hear from you. And I really mean it. I'm going to do another book so all my Dear Old Friends can help each other. So, write me about your problems with children, money, health, career, home, travel, clothes, house-cleaning, love affairs, everything and anything, and we'll share the wealth of your wisdom with all our Dear Old Friends across the country. We're going to all share a website titled, what else — DEAR OLD FRIENDS.

Oh, and I want to _repeat_ one last thought, because it's important and one I try to remember. When I'm facing a tough situation, or find myself getting angry at someone, or would really like to give someone a piece of my mind, I say to myself: "**Lord, put your arm around my shoulder and your hand over my mouth.**" Amen.

I look forward to hearing from all of you in the days and months and years ahead. To each of you, one and all, a big hug with much affection, from your Dear Old Friend, Jim. Wait, do you hear the band playing? May I have this dance?

Jim Flaherty
(James B. Flaherty)
P O Box 605 / Amenia, NY 12501
Or send me an email to:
talktome@jamesbflaherty.com
Again, here's my website: jamesbflaherty.com

About Author

"Hello, I'm Jim Flaherty, and I'd like to know you better."

Let's cut to the chase, friends. I'm a healthy, happy 86-year-old. Huh? Yep, 86, and don't mind it. Oh sure, it kind of annoys me I can't pound the table and say, "Well, I have 20 more good years." But gosh, I think it's great I've been gifted with 86 nonstop years and am still looking forward to a lot of tomorrows.

I was happy to grow up in Coral Gables, Florida, with my mid-Western parents and good public schools. I went to University of Florida in Gainesville (Go,Gators!) for my first two years of college, then graduated in 1957 from MSU, Michigan State University in East Lansing, with a degree in Communications.

The next twenty years were really satisfying. I did military service, married a beautiful girl, had two beautiful daughters, became an advertising copywriter, and surprised myself by ending up in the corner office, in NYC, earning more money I had ever dreamed of earning. Even enjoyed four executive years in Buenos Aires, Argentina.

I believed in the value of "shooting craps" with my life. Started a new business I knew nothing about at age 45, and Wow! It was successful. I created a country inn/conference center in a small town in the boonies—a huge risk—and it required at least 70 hours a week of nonstop work to make it happen. I think being The Innkeeper--psychiatrist, psychologist, boss, wedding planner, conference coordinator, best friend to guests who were there for business, romance, relaxing, or self-seeking, helped me understand what motivates people, and what is the inner motor that makes them win the race on that tough track called Life. Good stuff for a writer.

I also traveled a lot. Other cultures, other languages (I still speak Spanish fluently), other manners of living, even other climate zones, all work on your head and your hands (those fingers that type are very important).

Also, I'd really like to know you, better. If you will send me a note via email, I have a gift for you. There's a page in the front of the book that talks about that in more detail. I thought we might start some group meetings among those of us who understand the band won't stop playing till we stop dancing. Thanks for listening, friends. May I have the next dance?

Jim Flaherty.
Write me: **talktome@jamesbflaherty.com**.
We can become better acquainted if you visit My Website: **jamesbflaherty.com**

XO, Jim

Made in the USA
Middletown, DE
18 December 2021